FLAWED

Dr. James Byrd

No part of this publication may be reproduced, stored in retrieval system, transmitted in any form or by any means, electronic, mechanical, photo copying, recording, scanning, or otherwise, except as permitted under Section 107 or 108 of the United States Copyright Act, without either the prior written permission of the Publisher.

While the publisher and contributors/authors have used their best efforts in preparing this book, they make no representations or warranties with respect to the accuracy or completeness of the contents of this book and specifically disclaim any implied warranties of merchantability or fitness for a particular purpose. No warranty may be created or extended by the contributors/authors, implicitly or explicitly. The advice and strategies contained herein may not be suitable for your situation. Neither the publisher nor contributors/authors shall be liable for any loss of profit or any other commercial damages, including but not limited to special, incidental, consequential, or other damages.

Printed in the United States of America
Editing by Dr. James Byrd
Book Cover Design by John Lewis

Scripture taken from the Common English Bible®, CEB® Copyright © 2010, 2011 by Common English Bible.™ Used by permission. All rights reserved worldwide. The "CEB" and "Common English Bible" trademarks are registered in the United States Patent and Trademark Office by Common English Bible. Use of either trademark requires the permission of Common English Bible.

Dedication

To everyone who is married or thinking about getting married; *this* book is dedicated to you.

This book is dedicated to my earth Angel; Dr. Angel Byrd, my loving bride for the past 23 years. You have been my family partner, my business partner, my bedroom partner, my spiritual partner and you'll continue to be my partner for life.

To my Bishop, Dr. Steve Houpe, you were the first Godly man that I ever had a chance to glean from, and because of that, you became more than a Pastor, you became Dad

Foreword

Carey Casey

I believe your marriage will be forever changed and pointed in the right direction as you read this book, so appropriately entitled, *"Flawed, Marriage God's way is flawless, man's ways are flawed"*. I can still remember the first time I met Dr. James Byrd. He was sharing his vision of The Million Marriage Picnic, which is now a national, annual event. He was a young man that seemed eager to grow. His heart and passion burned for marriages and families all across the world.

James and his bride, Dr. Angel Byrd, have been married for almost 25 years and they pour their hearts and souls into helping marriages and families. As a couple, they are a wonderful representation of a Godly marriage. The Byrd's have so aptly been branded as "The Love Byrds." They are faith-based marriage and family counselors, authors, dynamic speakers, radio show hosts, and all-around good people.

This book, *Flawed,* is Dr. Byrd's attempt to turn around the failing marriages and alarming divorce rates in our society. Throughout time, man has inched further and further away from the likeness of God, and by doing so; marriages have continued to suffer. Not only are The Love Byrds living examples of how marriage works when doing it God's way, now they are sharing some of the most common areas where men and women have drifted away from God's original intent for marriage and putting us back on track. Enjoy, learn, and pass on the information from *Flawed*.

Carey Casey, CEO

National Center for Fathering

Carey Casey is Chief Executive Officer of the Kansas City based National Center for Fathering (NCF), with a vision to engage fathers or father figures in the life of every child. Prior to joining NCF, Carey worked for 18 years with the Fellowship of Christian Athletes including serving as president of the FCA Foundation. His career has included serving as an NFL team chaplain and as pastor of an inner-city church in urban Chicago. Carey serves on the White House Task Force on Fatherhood and Healthy Families. He is also a member of the executive committee of the National Fatherhood Leaders Group, which promotes responsible fatherhood policy, research, advocacy, and practice.

Table of Contents

Foreword	vi
Introduction	11
Chapter 1	
Why Get Married?	15
Chapter 2	
The First Wedding	27
Chapter 3	
A Tearing Away	35
Chapter 4	
J.C. Smashes the Law	45
Chapter 5	
Conjugal Visits	53
Chapter 6	
Time Divided	61
Chapter 7	
If It Don't Fit, You Must Get Rid of It	71
Chapter 8	
Sleeping with the Enemy	77
Chapter 9	
Whisper It, Submission	83
Chapter 10	
80/20 Rule	103
Chapter 11	
No "I" in Team	109
Chapter 12	
Remove That 2 x 4	115
Chapter 13	
Choose Them	123
Chapter 14	

Wow, Where Art Thou?	131
Chapter 15	
Guilty! 5 to 10	135
Chapter 16	
Do What I Say Woman!	139
Chapter 17	
Is It Love or Like?	147
Chapter 18	
Marriage Only Works Through Obedience	133
Conclusion	

Introduction

I was led to revisit an old movie titled *"Pretty Woman."* Watching the movie gave me a profound perspective I did not have before. The Lord showed me aspects of the movie that related to circumstances and mindsets in the lives of the man and woman portrayed in the two main characters.

Many of the marriages today are in serious condition. If marriages were in the hospital, most would be in the Intensive Care Unit. I am not telling you anything that you do not already know, especially if you are married. You could ask anyone over the age of eighteen, "What condition do you think marriages today are in." Most teens within that age group would tell you something close to what I have described. The divorce rates would back-up the statement as well. The statistics on infidelity in marriage support the increasing divorce rate. Many people today have the idea of not wanting to get married; this sentiment has increased in recent years. One of the reasons an 18 year-old would know about the state of marriage is from witnessing a flawed marriage at home. There is a great chance those under the age of 18 are being raised by a single parent and an even greater chance that if two parents are in the home, youth hear and see flaws in that relationship. Certainly, no marriage is without a single blemish. I caution you against using that as an excuse not to do something about the flaws in your own marriage. Just because no marriage is without a blemish, it does not give you an excuse to see the flaws in your marriage and do nothing about them.

There is only one thing to do with the flaws that you see in your relationship. That is to put a plan of action into place to work on them with the goal of removing them. Yes, one by one, you need to rid your marriage of its flaws. This may sound like a daunting task but think of it like this; if you aim for the moon and only reach the stars; you've still gone a long way and much further than most. I am ***attempting*** to get you to aim for the total removal of all the problems in your marriage.

"How do I determine what are the issues in my marriage which may cause a flaw?" you might ask. I'm glad you asked that. Herein lies the search you should conduct regarding your marriage relationship. This search may be impossible without the Word of God. Why the Word of God? That is an easy question to answer. When you get a brand new electronic device that you, your friends or family have never used before; how would you learn to operate it? There are a couple of ways to learn. First, you could use the old trial and error method. This method might result is some potential problems, or should I dare say flaws. The best way would be to read the instruction manual developed by the designer of the device. If they designed it, they would know best how to operate it at its optimal usage. The same is true of marriage. Marriage does have a designer, developer, maker, or should I say one who created it. That designer is God. Not only did He create marriage, but also he wrote an instruction manual to go along with it.

The Bible is man's instruction manual to living and it is man's guide for relationships. Marriage is the numero uno[1] relationship on the earth. I hope you like that bilingual approach of mine. We are going to take a journey through the

---

[1] "number one" in Spanish

marriage instruction manual as it relates to flawed marriages in today's society. Of course, we won't touch on every instruction to relationships in this one book, but we'll get off to a good start. I pray that you enjoy "Flawed" and better yet, I pray that you begin to attack the flaws in your relationship.

Chapter 1
Why Get Married?

*^{18} Then the L*ORD *God said, "It's not good that the human is alone. I will make him a helper that is perfect for him."* Genesis 2:18 Common English Bible (CEB)

The purpose of this book is to walk you through Scriptures, which speak directly to marriage, or can be easily used to influence your marriage union. You will frequently hear me refer to God as the Author and Creator of marriage. Anyone who creates the universe, the heavens, and the earth surely has the intelligence to provide the necessary directions and instructions for all He has created. Since, God created everything, that would make His way flawless and any other way potentially FLAWED; thus the title of this writing!

We will discover just how far man has drifted away from God's flawless instructions for this relationship called marriage. We will make every **attempt** to guide you to God as the foremost authority on marriage. While speaking at events or live on the radio, you will often hear me say nine words that I came up with by the inspiration of the Holy Spirit; and that is "*God's way is **flawless and** man's ways are **flawed**.*" Concentrating on the theme that God created everything, including humans, supports the Scripture where He said, *"It's not good for man to be alone."* I will take a chance and just agree with God. I believe He knew that something was needed for man, and that man could not achieve it in his aloneness. I am saying from personal experience that my growth as a married man has been something I could not have achieved had I remained single. When we think about that statement, we often think of things like monetary achievements or having children. Those are obvious things, but I'm not referring to just those types of things. I am talking about things like learning to be concerned about the feelings of another over those of your own. For example, being there in the time of need for someone; running errands when you really cannot and do not feel like it, and canceling the activities that you enjoy for the betterment of your relationship.

These are all factors that you develop in a relationship that begin while you are single or dating. When you are single, it is much tougher to grow in these areas. I am not totally ruling out you being able to experience growth in these areas, but you do not experience them in the face of the type of extreme heat that the fire of marriage brings. As a single person, you are more likely to grow in talent, skill and abilities but you cannot grow in areas that are forced by the challenges of another human being; who happens to be closer to you than anyone has ever been in your entire life. There are obvious levels that man can only reach through the marriage relationship.

Marriage brings out the character in us and helps us develop the God kind of love that is hidden inside every spirit-filled believer. This kind of development evolves through relationships, and there is no greater relationship in the physical than that of a husband and his wife. There is no other challenging relationship as that of the marriage relationship. On any given day, you might confess that you will die for your spouse. Within a timeframe of weeks, months, or even years, you may develop hatred in your heart for the person in which you were willing to die. Believe me; I am not saying it's the only relationship that you can develop and grow within. You surely can develop character within the relationship of a child to a parent or a mentee to an adult. You can even develop character from a supervisor/manager to an employee relationship at work. However, it takes someone who is married to tell you how challenging the marriage relationship can be. If you have never been married, there are no amount of stories or movies that can simulate the potential highs and lows of the marriage relationship. Marriage has something to do with the high expectations that are put on couples and the disappointments when those expectations are not met. When a couple stands at the altar vowing their love for each other, the expectations of the relationship and the expectations of his/her spouse can be tremendous. The expectations between each other do not take very long to become disappointments. One thing, which rips away at a marriage, is unmet expectations. Some expectations are unrealistic but if anticipated, they will eventually turn into disappointments when they are consistently unmet. I used to tell my lovely bride that she expected every day to be at 100 percent. We referred to disagreements or issues between us as growth challenges. I felt this way because of how hard she took disagreements when we would have them. It is not just her; I had and still have expectations that at times are not legitimate.

Some expectations are brought into a marriage from the perspective of what you have watched on television, heard in locker rooms, beauty salons, school busses, or cafeterias. You have to be careful not to put these unrealistic expectations on your spouse but to put the expectations that God our creator has of them. Even then, you have to be careful and patient with Godly expectations. If your spouse is not meeting the expectations God has put on them, that is another challenge and the Word of God is the place to grow in all aspects as a man and a woman. There are some expectations that if not met would be deal breakers. Deal breakers refer to those things that would cause one not to marry a person if they did not already have the victory over the problem. We will talk more about this as we get further along in upcoming chapters.

God is clearly letting us know how He expects His creation to form the marriage union. He makes a helpmate suitable for the man. This helpmate would suit him intellectually, morally, and would be his physical counterpart. I believe that the physical way He made us male and female, makes it clear what His flawless intentions were for us where marriage is concerned. Anyone who would try to say that God is o.k. with man on man or woman on woman relationships is ignoring the obvious physical way that He created us and that would be a FLAWED way of thinking. God knows that for His greatest creation to thrive in the way He had in mind, man would need to come together in marriage and grow through the development that only the marriage relationship could bring. The original woman (Eve) was created by God from the original man (Adam) to be the help that he needed to, shall I dare say, <u>be all that he can be</u>, if I can borrow that phrase from the Army. I know personally without any doubt that I would not be close to who I am now if it was not for my marriage to my lovely wife

Dr. Angel Byrd. So I guess what I am saying is, if you do not like me, or what I have become, you can blame it on her. Of course I am just kidding, but she has helped me to become more than I could have even imagined I could have become, and I'd like to think I've done the same for her. Now again, if you don't like her and who she has become, I guess you can blame me. It is literally amazing how God can join two individuals together and one can have in them exactly what the other needs and vice versa. It seems as if everything I lacked was in her and everything she needed was in me. You really don't notice it at the beginning because you are too busy trying to romance each other, and do the things you enjoy that fit into the compatibility department between the two of you. You tell everyone how much you are alike and how much you have in common, when in all actuality there are many more things about you that are different. However, at some point, reality sets in and those differences in you start to surface; such as one spouse being neat, and the other not so much. I said that in a way that was nice when in all actuality many marriages are usually put together with a neat freak, and should I say a person that doesn't care as much about that part of life. Within a marriage relationship, you also have one spouse who may be aggressive and the other spouse laid back. This is a good example because during the dating phase the aggressive one loves the fact that the other is so calm under pressure and so reserved. The reserved one loves the fact that the other is such a go-getter and helps them to do more than they would normally do. At least they feel that way until trouble arises and the aggressive one wants the reserved one to move a lot quicker. This also works for the times when the aggressive one is doing too much, and the laid-back mate needs them to slow their roll. It is also the same for the couple that is made up of one who is usually afraid of risk, and the other a risk taker.

When one is calm under pressure, and the other is a hothead, this will probably create problems later on down the line. The problems that come along with these differences, usually surface before the ecstasy stage has faded away. In fact, this difference possibly has a lot to do with ecstasy fading away. We all have taken it for granted that the ecstasy in marriage has to fade away eventually, thus we refer to it as a stage or phase of the relationship. However, I tend to disagree with this assumption because twenty-three years into marriage I am still in the ecstasy phase of my marriage, so if this is a phase it doesn't appear to be going away anytime soon, if at all. As you can see this list of differences could seemingly go on. This is why the marriage relationship is at least the best relationship to literally, force you to grow closer or you will unknowingly grow apart. If you do it God's way, you will unquestionably grow together, but if you choose man's FLAWED way, you most likely will grow apart. Remember God's way is flawless and man's ways are flawed. You will grow so far apart doing it man's way that the "D" word usually sets in. I don't like saying that word in the context of marriage, but for the sake of the book, the "D" word refers to divorce, and it will come knocking on your door. The horrible thing about choosing man's way over God's, is that it only takes one person in a relationship not willing to do it God's way to lead to the demise of the marriage. I will however say that if the other spouse is willing to choose God's way, they can still achieve great levels of development in their love walk and character. To be honest with you, the most development you can possibly make is when you have to follow God's ways while your spouse is not willing to walk down that same road. Sometimes your spouse will even seem to jump on board with Satan himself, and that is a hard road for any believer to travel. My heart goes out to people whenever we counsel couples that are in this situation. Most of the time when this situation presents itself in marriage, there is no need to counsel both the man and the woman. It would probably be best to counsel the one that is trying to walk the path of Christ. If one of them is not willing to do it God's way, the "D" word may be inevitable unless the believing spouse is willing to pray and wait for a change. The change does not always come, sorry to say, and depending on how far one walks away from God will determine the path that the believing spouse must take. We will talk later about how and why God hates divorce, and how it was clearly never apart of His original plan or flawless intent for the marriage relationship. Did I just write His original plan and flawless intent for the marriage relationship!?! Now there is a noble idea. Maybe that is why we should look to get married in the first place.

People get married for all kinds of reasons today, but not many people get married for God's original plan and intent. You will see later why God wanted you to marry and what His plan was all along. "But Dr. Byrd," you say, "We are already married and yeah it wasn't originally for the right reasons, but now that we are married, how do we avoid the "D" word?" I believe a helpmate suitable for man along with a man operating in God's original intent, will never get a divorce. My Bishop, Dr. Steve Houpe, would always say, "Two born again believers operating in the love of God will never get a divorce." What he was saying is that too much love would be present and too much fulfillment would take place to consider tearing that union apart. These types of individuals are more concerned with pleasing God and pleasing their spouse rather than hurting them or disappointing them. I am willing to go on record and in print to profess that no man operating in God's intent and purpose for his life which includes love that dies for his wife, along with a woman operating in God's intent as a help mate which includes honoring and respecting that kind of man, have or will ever get a divorce. I would say the roles of the relationship God has set in place as it relates to man vs. woman, have to become more balanced. The man who is the head in the relationship needs to allow his helper to help. She is not just there to raise the kids or meet his physical needs, but God has put the two of them together for a specific plan to fulfill in the earth. If you, the male, don't allow her to be the help meet she was created to be, that's where separation can come in to play and most couples tend to grow apart and resentment sets in because you are not allowing the others gift to surface in the relationship. In addition, I do not think there should be any competition or jealousy in the relationship as it relates to your gifts. As you grow and get the plan of God for your marriage, you both will find out what those gifts are and they will surface. Then encourage each other on their respective gifts and those gifts will flourish and work together for the good of the marriage.

Finally, if you're reading this and your current circumstances are not that of God's original intent for marriage, my advice to you would be; first to keep reading, and second to start right where you are. Begin to operate at this moment-in-time as close to God's original plan as possible. God's grace is sufficient and He will forgive you of your past.

Chapter 2
The First Wedding

²¹ So the L<small>ORD</small> God put the human into a deep and heavy sleep, and took one of his ribs and closed up the flesh over it. ²² With the rib taken from the human, the L<small>ORD</small> God fashioned a woman and brought her to the human being.

²³ The human said, "This one finally is bone from my bones and flesh from my flesh. She will be called a woman because from a man she was taken."²⁴ This is the reason that a man leaves his father and mother and embraces his wife, and they become one flesh. Genesis 2:21-24 (CEB)

Ahhhhhh; the marriage ceremony! So much time, effort, energy, and thought goes into the marriage ceremony. There are many tremendous marriage rituals and ceremonies today. From the basic wedding before a judge or in a private pastor's chamber, to millions of dollars spent by some of the richest people in the world. Jumping the broom is done in so many different ways. You can travel the world and see the beauty and extravagance placed into the marriage ceremony. There have even been reality television shows that rival lifestyles of the rich and famous and MTV[2] cribs about nothing but fabulous weddings. The budgets for some of these weddings are more than many couples make in ten years! While some seemingly take the wedding over the top, others do not take it seriously enough. I often wonder how a marriage is going to go when

---

[2] MTV is the acronym for Music Television

I see the wedding set up like a joke or some kind of comedy show. What is the happy medium or normalcy that we should expect in a marriage ceremony? I can't tell you one is right or one is wrong. Whichever way people choose to do the ceremonies today is not the real point.

The original foundation for marriage was laid in the very beginning and that is the point of the wedding. The wedding is to announce to our families and friends that we are joining in covenant and we want the world to know it. God laid the foundation for one flesh marriage by creating woman from man to be his helpmate. Whatever way you decide to put that into action, you must agree that it is serious business and not something that should be taken lightly. This sounds like a line from the marriage wedding vows, along with for richer or poorer, in sickness and in health, and as long as we both shall live. If we say these vows and we hear these vows, why don't we believe these vows, and why don't we keep these vows? I am going to leave the creativity of the ceremony up to you, but know that God does and says everything for a reason. He said that in the beginning he took the woman from the man. God needed to separate man for the purpose of procreation, domination, and expressing His love in the earth. Let us look at these three.

(1). Procreation is easy to recognize and understand. Simply look below the waistline of the male and female, and all your questions will be answered. There is not much for you to be confused. That alone kills the theory that some are born homosexual or lesbian. To think that, would be to think that God makes mistakes and we know that is not true.

(2). Domination is not what it seems to be when you take that word in the way most people use it in our society today. This is not man dominating his wife or vice versa, this is about agreement and what you can do together, that you cannot do apart so that you can dominate or have dominion in those things God called us to have dominion over. It is in your union that you put two people with dominion together, that gives more God given power and authority.

Finally, (3) expressing God's love in the earth is what marriage is supposed to model or reflect. Although God separated the human when he took woman from the man, He wanted them to operate as one flesh and express His love in the earth. We can't express God's love if we are alone, but together in marriage we can give a picture of His love every day of our lives. Satan does everything he can to destroy this one flesh relationship. He does not want us to procreate, dominate, or express God's love. Even Satan knows that God's plan was flawless if carried out correctly and efficiently. That is why right from the very first marriage of Adam and Eve he put his attack on the institution of marriage. God meant for humans to exemplify to one another the type of love

God Himself would ultimately express through the sacrifice of His only Son.

Satan has set out to destroy the institution of marriage and has succeeded in many cases in convincing man that marriage is archaic and no longer needed. Satan has even convinced many that they get along better when they just cohabitate vs. doing it God's way and striking covenant. He has also convinced many that in relationships men and women cannot get along, so they have moved into having alternative relationships. There are men together with men and women together with women both occurring at an all-time high. This is a lie from the father of lies, Satan himself. This is nothing new or original. Satan has been pulling that same deception since the early days of humankind, God was against it then, and He is still against it now. Don't get me wrong, God loves the people, all of the people He created, but He despises these wicked actions. The wickedness is about Satan trying to foil every plan of God, and if he has tricked you into accepting this; you are a pawn in Satan's chess game against everything God stands for.

I am personally not okay with homosexuality or lesbianism, but I can say that after you see something so many times you start to be desensitized to it. There was once a time that if I saw a woman kissing another woman I would almost get sick to my stomach, but after having it thrown in your face on television, in the movies, or just being out for an evening stroll, I sometimes pay no attention to it at all. As a believer, I don't want to have the "pay no attention to it" attitude. I need to have the *pray for them,* and *pray for marriages* in our society attitude. The more successful loving, traditional marriages we have, the less opportunity for that spirit to gain momentum. Satan is using people to get back at God. Satan knows that with homosexuality and lesbianism, you will never get out of the marriage relationship what the Creator of marriage had in mind. Satan has even convinced man to come up with ways to circumvent the natural procreation of marriage. Regardless of the inventions of man, God's way to grow His family has always been man and woman together in holy matrimony and that will always be God's flawless way. Always remember that whenever you want to know the purpose of something, the creator of that something is the best source. God is the Creator of marriage, so that makes God the best source on marriage and its purpose, not Satan and definitely not you and me.

I once told my wife that after reading this passage of Scripture, I envisioned a marriage ceremony today in which the man is asked to close his eyes in representation of God putting him to sleep in the garden. He would then be touched by the officiator of the ceremony, on his side and asked to visualize his wife being taken from inside of him. She would then come down the aisle and he would leave his father and mother and cleave to his wife. He would thus always have a visual reminder of God's original intent for marriage. I get a little emotional just thinking about how spiritual a ceremony that would be. Marriage should be this serious, and not the way it is in some places today where it has become a joke. If you are not careful, you will fall into this trap as if I have a time or two in my past. The institution of marriage is no joke and the ceremony that joins two to become one should not be either.

If you're married today and you ever decide to redo your wedding vows, think about making it as special as what I've written above. If you are not yet married, you have a perfect opportunity to make it special the very first and only time. Today make a new commitment to become a one-flesh union. Men cleave to your wives. Leave your parents, friends, job, televisions, and whatever else gets in the way and become a cleaving one-flesh marriage union.

All of these distractions are viewed as flaws in today's marriages. To all men, your wife will follow a man like this. Only a woman who is not in her right mind would be able to resist such a man. You notice God didn't have to tell her to leave and cleave. This is something that God put into woman. Any woman, who would run from her husband if he were operating the way I have described, would be doing so based upon past disappointments in her life. Maybe it is something she learned from the relationship between her and her father. Perhaps it stems from the lack of a relationship between her and her father! Maybe it is hurt and distrust from a previous relationship. No matter what it is, God's man has the ability with the God kind of love to love her back to wholeness, security, and trust. Will you be that kind of man? Will you be God's original kind of woman? Anything less is FLAWED.

Chapter 3
A Tearing Away

¹⁴But you say, "Why?" Because the LORD testifies about you and the wife of your youth against whom you cheated. She is your partner, the wife of your covenant.¹⁵ Didn't he make her the one and the remnant of his spirit? What is the one? The one seeking godly offspring; you should guard your own spirit. Don't cheat on the wife of your youth ¹⁶ because he hates divorce, says the LORD God of Israel, and he also hates the one covering his garment with violence, says the LORD of heavenly

forces. Guard your own life, and don't cheat. Malachi 2:14-16 Common English Bible (CEB)

God's original plan was for our marriage to be a one-flesh union, and we were never supposed to deal treacherously with our spouse. Listen to the description of the word treacherously in the text. Treacherous is an adjective characterized by faithlessness or readiness to betray trust, traitorous, deceptive, untrustworthy, unreliable, unstable or insecure as footing. I believe the only word left out in this definition was FLAWED. This statement was obviously being directed at men. During that time men were divorcing their wives for any and every reason. In today's world, it would be for reasons as; "She doesn't light my fire anymore," or something like "We've fallen out of love and I just don't love her anymore." These are ridiculously shallow reasons to wind up in divorce, especially when feelings fluctuate. Just as you once felt in love and now you don't, you can also again regain and feel those feelings. I know you might not think so when you're in a bad place in your marriage, but there are many couples who have recovered the feelings of love and intimacy. This has happened after being in a hard place and facing divorce.

There are couples who after divorce have remarried and now have the feeling of the love they had when they first met. I am not advocating feelings as the glue to your marriage, because love is a decision, and should never be based on a feeling. However, feelings do make it either easier, or more difficult to follow your decision to love. Again, divorce was never God's original plan for His highest creation and that is how you must look at yourself, as God's highest creation. Let us take another look at this word treacherously that the Bible used here. Again the Webster's dictionary defines it as faithlessness or readiness to betray trust, traitorous, deceptive, untrustworthy, unreliable, unstable, insecure footing, dangerous, hazardous, deceitful, and treasonous. I think now you can see why God would not want us dealing treacherously with the wife of our youth or the wife you have chosen.

I took the word treacherously from the New King James Version because it shines a light on us if we start to walk away from the covenant we made at the altar or in a judges chamber. The King James Version reads; *Yet you say, "For what reason?" Because the LORD has been witness between you and the wife of your youth, with whom you have dealt treacherously, yet she is your companion and your wife by covenant.* The prophet Malachi in this passage also tells us that God hates divorce. Hate is the strongest word he could have used here. Hate is referred to as an antonym for love and we know that God is love so hate is the opposite of God. You might say I don't hate my spouse to that degree, but anyone who has been married and had children will surely tell you why God hates divorce.

A divorce causes so much hurt and pain. Not only does it cause pain to the husband and wife but also to any of their offspring. It tears and rips away at the very fabric of the family. When two are joined together, they become one, and when you tear something apart that is one; it now becomes fragmented, jaded, ripped, and torn. Think about two sheets of paper that you glue together and let that glue settle in for a year or two. Now try to separate the two sheets of paper. The two sheets that you once had would now be fragmented in such a way, that pieces of one sheet would still be part of the other sheet. The affect divorce has on a couple can't be summarized in the chapters of an entire book! Divorce is often described as being worse than the death of a spouse, because the death of a spouse is final, because you do not see them anymore. However, with divorce you often see them on a weekly, bi-weekly or monthly basis with a constant reminder of what has happened. Looking at the children is also a constant reminder. As if that is not bad enough, think about what it does to the children the couple has produced. Children often blame themselves for a divorce and sometimes never recover from the issues that it brings them psychologically. Many children of divorced parents wind up not trusting their spouse and eventually divorcing themselves.

Divorce is a multiplication system used by the devil to work against God's plan to multiply with Godly offspring. Divorce is definitely a flaw in the marriage relationship. I personally don't have to look very far to see the manifestation of a divorce. My parents divorced when I was just thirteen years old, and I never saw or interacted with my father for all of my teenage years. Sure, I seemed to be all right. I was a very good athlete and popular kid, but I had no idea of what I was missing in terms of becoming a man without my father in my life. I also had no image that was tangible to give me a snap shot of marriage. Sometimes you don't know that you're missing something until later on in life when you need to draw on it and it is nowhere in your reservoir.

I grew up with television characters, as my model for marriage and with those models, there was never any serious quarreling. On television, if there were disagreements, they were usually settled within a 30-minute period or shortly after a commercial break. By the time I said "I DO" to my beautiful bride, I soon realized that "I DO" really was just part of what I was saying. The rest of it went something like "I DO not know what I am doing". I loved my Angel, but I didn't know how to express it because I never saw a man express love. I didn't know how to cater to my wife because I never saw a man cater to a woman. I didn't know how to provide for a woman because I never saw a man totally provide for his wife. I never knew how to teach my wife the word of God because I never saw a man teach his wife the word. I never knew how to resolve conflict in a healthy manner because I never saw it demonstrated.

Now you can really start to see why God hates divorce because it takes away His model plan for child rearing. My upbringing was FLAWED. Most of the things I just mentioned, that I didn't know, were introduced to me after I said I DO, by the man

I grew to love as my spiritual father Bishop Steve Houpe. Don't get me wrong, I'm not saying that my father didn't possess any of those characteristics, but I am saying because of the divorce I never saw it. In my memories, my dad was not a bad man. He seemed to always work and keep a job. He was an over the road truck driver. He worked hard but so did my mom and after the divorce I remembered her working more than one job to provide for my brothers and I. As an adult, I have repaired the relationship with my dad and he is now a faithful believer who serves in the house of God. Even though I repaired the relationship with my father, it did not take away from what the divorce did while I was a child. As I write this book, the effects of the divorce were much worse on my younger brothers because they were only seven and a year-old.

My wife also is a divorce survivor and her parents divorced when she was just a child, so she too had negative effects of a divorce as a molder of her character growing up. We always say that there is no way possible that we would still be together if we did not have God as the center of our lives. Only God can take two individuals with a FLAWED upbringing and turn them into "The Love Byrd's." God's Word sustained us, especially early on in the marriage when it was extremely difficult to get along. The Word of God and believing in the covenant of marriage has thrust us in to something we wouldn't have dreamed possible long ago, even two years into our marriage.

In verse 15 there is another point I want to bring to your attention and that is where Malachi said, the whole point of the one flesh marriage unit is reproduction, because God was seeking Godly seed. God wants to produce more and more children that will live for Him, follow Him, serve Him, and make this world a better place to live. If we produce this kind of seed and they in turn do the same thing, we would be instituting God's flawless plan to recover his family. You often hear people complain about the world we live in or the problems in our country, and even the schools or neighborhoods. We all want things to change for the better but in order to accomplish this, God is expecting us to demonstrate His love to our spouses and our children so they won't have the same testimony that we had as children. Obviously, I am proof that you can overcome it, but you have to go through unnecessary hardship to overcome something that could have easily been deposited in you as you grew up. If you want things in this world to change, we have to bring His Kingdom to earth.

This is how to see God's Kingdom come and His will be done on earth as it is in heaven. Remember, Satan is out to foil every plan of God. He started with marriage and knew that if he could keep sin in the hearts and minds of man he would put a dent in God's plan for us to produce Godly offspring. Sometimes we think about so many things we want to see, and produce in our kids, instead of the Godly side, which is the most important. Just think about the difference in the life of a child that is cultivated in an environment that reflects the attributes of God's love, versus a child cultivated in a home of chaos, confusion, strife, separation, selfishness or divorce. The finished product could be as different as night and day. God is after one-flesh marriages that produce Godly offspring. The purpose of marriage has just been presented for you. For everyone reading this book, it's up to you to play this game on God's team, or to join Satan on the losing squad. I know it may seem that Satan's team is winning right now with all of the divorces and domestic issues we hear about, but things are not always, as they appear. I have insight on the end of this game and Satan and his team will flat out lose.

Chapter 4
J.C. Smashes the Law

³ Some Pharisees came to him. In order to test him, they said, "Does the Law allow a man to divorce his wife for just any reason ⁴ Jesus answered, "Haven't you read that at the beginning the creator made them male and female? ⁵ And God said, 'Because of this a man should leave his father and mother and be joined together with his wife, and the two will be one flesh. ⁶ So they are no longer two but one flesh. Therefore, humans must not pull apart what God has put together." ⁷ The Pharisees said to him, "Then why did Moses command us to give a divorce certificate and divorce her?"⁸ Jesus replied, "Moses allowed you to divorce your wives because your hearts are unyielding. But it wasn't that way from the beginning.⁹ I say to you that whoever divorces his wife, except for sexual unfaithfulness, and marries another woman commits adultery." Matthew 19:3-9 Common English Bible (CEB)

Are you seeing a consistent theme? Jesus is pointing you back to God's original intent for marriage. Don't you see it clearly jumping off the pages of the Scriptures? The very reason God separated man from woman, was for the intent and purpose of marriage alone, the one-flesh marriage. God designed all of us to be raised by a father and mother, and then at some point leave them and cleave to your spouse. Yes, I know it says for a man to leave and cleave, but if we use reasoning, we'll understand that if the man leaves and cleaves, the woman he's cleaving to must also. God certainly wasn't talking about him leaving his parents and staying with his wife and her parents or cleaving to all of them. They had to cling together. Marriage was always about togetherness, oneness, and unions. The Scripture is presented the way it is because God always gave instructions to the male in the beginning. The male was to lead and guide his family in all things pertaining to life and godliness. We should always go back to the beginning to see God's original intent. Look at it this way. Usually anything in life that you find out of order, can soon be back in order and running smoothly if you just get it back to the original order of God. If you are playing basketball and twist your ankle, wear braces, keep the pressure off it, you can in time, find yourself back playing basketball without pain.

Another example of returning order is the automobile. The best mechanics are the ones who can get your car running like new again. These mechanics are trained and authorized by the manufacturer to work on the car with authorized parts. Sometimes you'll try to take a short cut and use a shade tree mechanic who will get your car running, but they are not trained and authorized by the manufacturer and they don't always use authorized parts. They finagle a part here or there, and take a piece out that they'll say wasn't really needed and before you know it, the car is back down again, and probably going to cost you more money. If you would have gone the manufacturers route in the first place, the automobile would have been less costly. This type of mechanic is FLAWED. I am reminded of a time I once decided that I would change the radiator in one of our vehicles. Now you might think, "What's the big deal" with someone changing his or her own radiator. This is laughable if you know me because I'm not the kind of guy that fixes cars. I usually stop at adding gas, oil, other fluids, and changing tires. Imagine a rookie trying to fix a radiator. I went and I picked up a new radiator from the auto shop and took it to my mom's house. My dad was there working on another vehicle. This was the smartest part of my plan because he is the one that works on vehicles all the time. I once remember my dad completely taking an engine apart and putting it back together again. I felt that if he was at least there on the scene it was worth the risk because he could help with any issues I might run into. First things first, I removed the old radiator and very carefully placed all the pieces I removed in one spot, so I would remember where to put them back. I was able to get the old radiator out and the new one in place. I then placed fluid in the radiator and afterwards I thought everything was o.k.

I felt good about myself being able to do engine work. Perhaps a work-on-car gene that passed down from my dad and it just took a while to develop in me. One thing I didn't mention was that because of where the radiator was I had to remove the latch which closes the hood of the vehicle and reinstall it once the new part was in. I got everything back in place and closed the hood and to my surprise, it would not latch. I thought I had put everything back to its original place and purpose but the slightest mistake caused something not to work.

It wasn't until I removed the latch again, turned it around and put it back properly that I was able to shut the hood and ride away. Sometimes things have to be exactly the way they were originally intended to be, and that definitely goes for the things God has created. The point here is the same point Jesus was making. Man tries to do things his own flawed way, but from the beginning, God's way was not flawed. Let's just get back to the one-flesh, leave and cleave, kind of Agape love and stop dealing treacherously with our spouses. Remember the vows you made. You made a covenant with God and your spouse before witnesses. I really believe we need to teach couples during premarital counseling a lot more in detail what this covenant they are making really consists of. The line you repeat in the marriage that says, "*until death we part*" is the line that refers to the marriage covenant. A covenant is not broken unless one of the parties dies. You can't just decide to break a covenant over irreconcilable differences or because you've lost that loving feeling. You had better fix the differences and find that feeling again. Just as you can get a sprained ankle back to new again, and your automobile running like new again, so too can you find the loving feelings you've lost in a marriage relationship. The secret is in the words "one flesh." Whenever you can get a husband and wife operating as one unit in agreement with each other, those loving feelings will soon return and many times stronger than ever.

    We need to teach more on the meaning of love and the love God intended for us to operate in. We are only able to share something if we have it to give. I can't give you a million dollars if I don't have a million dollars. I cannot give you a big screen television if I don't have one to give. I cannot give you a ride across the Atlantic Ocean if I don't have an airplane or a boat and we can't give love if we don't have it to give. God is love and if we do not have God we can't give love. The scary thing about it is we sometimes think we are giving God's love but our actions say otherwise. Look back at your fruit and that will tell you if you are giving love. The type of love I am referring to is the Agape love. You can't judge it by how you feel. We need to focus on the 1 Corinthians 13:4-7 love. This kind of love says that we should be patient, kind, not jealous or rude, not boastful, not proud, not demanding of our own way, and not irritable. We should not keep a record of wrongs done to us, never give up or lose faith, but we should be hopeful and endure together through every circumstance. Is this what your track record of love is showing? If it is not, you have some work to do in the area of love. This is what one flesh, back to the beginning, leaving and cleaving, Agape love is all about. This was God's way, this was Jesus' way, and if you want my opinion, this is my way.

Chapter 5
Conjugal Visits

[1]Now, about what you wrote: "It's good for a man not to have sex with a woman."[2] Each man should have his own wife, and each woman should have her own husband because of sexual immorality.[3] The husband should meet his wife's sexual needs, and the wife should do the same for her husband.[4] The wife doesn't have authority over her own body, but the husband does. Likewise, the husband doesn't have authority over his own body, but the wife does.[5] Don't refuse to meet each other's

needs unless you both agree for a short period of time to devote yourselves to prayer. Then come back together again so that Satan might not tempt you because of your lack of self-control. 1 Corinthians 7:1-5 Common English Bible (CEB)

I am resisting the urge to start on the part of this passage that many have twisted for their own benefit. I believe we are clearly instructed by this passage of text to avoid fornication. The sin of fornication has become so prevalent in society today that many people don't even think it is a sin anymore. All you hear is, "God understands." Many confessing Christians have even adopted the world's views as it relates to fornication. Many believe that as long as I'm only fornicating with one person and I feel like I love them, everything is all right between me and my God. Many people use the term *my God* as if God has a special set of rules for them that don't apply to everyone else. We often hear such excuses as the following; "my God is loving as well as forgiving, and He understands.

My intentions are to get married one day; we are just waiting for the right time. Our relationship is good like it is and we don't want marriage to mess it up right now. Some have been married and will use the excuse that it didn't work so they are afraid to try it again. Some were raised with parents that had a bad marriage and they are afraid to repeat the cycle. Some women are afraid that if they hold up a standard for marriage they will miss meeting a man and end up alone. They fear the statistics of how many more women there are than men and they settle for sex outside of covenant. For whatever the reason, it's amazing how man's flawed ways have become so popular and God's flawless ways have become extinct or old fashioned. Could you imagine the state of those who think like this if the same attitude were used with their employers? The company rules are to begin work on time, do your work assigned for an agreed upon salary. You decide that you'll show up late sometimes as long as you seemingly do good work. Well you might think that the company will understand that you have kids to support and things happen from time to time. However, what's going to happen is that employer sings the song of the famous Donald Trump. "You're fired." If you did the research on the success rate of those doing it their own way when it comes to marriage God's way versus fornication, the numbers would literally cause your jaw to hit the floor. Statistics say that for every ten couples that started out cohabitating and fornicating, nine of them never make it to the altar. Of the 10% that do get married, 80% of them end in divorce. Those are some dismal statistics for doing it man's way versus God's way. That means that if you are one of those women that think holding out hurts your chances of getting married; statistically you have it all wrong because sex before marriage actually lessens your chances at getting married especially at having a successful marriage. Even though man's ways are all over television, movies, music and gossip columns, there is no success achieved with marriage done man's way.

A lot of broken hearts and disappointments are leaving singles in a bad state, so that when they do get married, they take all that damage and negativity into their marriage. Even though mostly married couples are probably reading this book, I cannot help but share with the wise singles that are reading marriage books in preparation for that big day. We see this on a regular basis in our **Flourishing Marriages Counseling** practice, where men and women are trying to work it out, but they have so many of the hurts and pains of the past surfacing in their current marriages. Painful relationships cause so much distrust and it causes so many walls to build even amongst married couples.

Next, it's clear every man should have his own wife and every woman her own husband. All of this lusting after everything that floats your boat or giving pieces of your soul to another person complicates your ability to love your spouse unconditionally without unrealistic expectations. Some of the expectations that people have going into marriage with these days are coming from things experienced in the world while engaging in sin. Some have even taken things from watching pornography into what is supposed to be a holy union. These are not the type of expectations to bring into God's holy union. The expectations you should have for your spouse should come from the Word of God and time spent together. You should learn and experience each other together. The expectations you have for each other will develop from the time spent together.

Now, the expectations that you should have concerning your bodies is clear from the Scriptures. The husband's body belongs to her and the wife's body belongs to him. I can pretty much tell what you're thinking when you read this based on your age. Most young men are thinking WOW I get to have as much sex as I want while most young women are thinking MAN I have to give it to him as much as he wants. If you are older, most older men are still thinking; I get to have sex as much as I want, while most older women have changed and are now thinking that I get to have it as much as I want. I don't want you to get this twisted! This is not a license for you to be abusive, demanding, selfish, and un-loving. This premise is better understood in this manner. "My body is not my own, so I offer it willingly to my wife and her body is not hers so she offers it willingly to me." If I do not really feel like it, I should get in the Word, adjust my attitude, and give it willingly. A wife should not demand it and force me through clever use of words. If I am always willing and she is always willing we will never have an issue in this area of our marriage.

This is very different from what most people think about with this Scripture. You see most people think about themselves when they read this, instead of thinking about their mate. When I read the Scripture, my wife's body is not her own but it belongs to me. The Scriptural reference should spark me to treat her body with tender love and care and not just to think about how often I can have sex. You see this area of your marriage has the power to keep you strong against the temptations of Satan; when the two of you are using it to make love and satisfy each other, and not to fulfill some sick twisted fantasies. Unfortunately, many have let the lust of this world and what the world parades in our faces as love and sex become the standards for marriage today. The problem with this is that standard does not run the devil off from your marriage. That standard enhances the devils attack in your life. It leaves you unfulfilled as a woman and open to the doors of lust and pornography as a man. These wrong thoughts can lead to relationships outside of your covenant of marriage and can lead to all kinds of problems particularly if there are children in the picture. You must remember that whenever we are talking about problems in marriage and doing things outside of God's directions for your marriage, you open the door for all kinds of evil that hurts not only you but the one who has hurt you. It spills over into the families that have come to know your spouse. It flows over into the church friends and families that have come to know your spouse. It flows over into every relationship that the two of you have come to know and love. When you are hurting in your relationship and you divorce as a way out, you hurt far more than the spouse you think has hurt you. You must treat each other's bodies with tender love and care and use sex as a tool to bring you closer together and not let it become a wedge of separation.

Chapter 6
Time Divided

³² I want you to be free from concerns. A man who isn't married is concerned about the Lord's concerns—how he can please the Lord. ³³ But a married man is concerned about the world's concerns—how he can please his wife. ³⁴ His attention is divided. A woman who isn't married or who is a virgin is concerned about the Lord's concerns so that she can be dedicated to God in both body and spirit. But a married woman is concerned about the world's concerns—how she can please her husband. 1 Corinthians 7:32-34 Common English Bible (CEB)

This passage is not talked about much, but I believe it is saying a whole lot. First, one of the reasons singles are finding themselves struggling in their walk in the Spirit, is because they are acting and thinking in ways that only married folk should think. Singles should be devoting their time, energy, and effort into pleasing the Lord. You might wonder what it looks like to devote everything to the Lord in today's times. Here is one way to look at it, we call it the God first principle from Matthew 6:33 (*But seek ye first the Kingdom of God, and its righteousness; and all these things shall be added unto you.*) Everyone has what I like to call me time, or your own personal time. Let me break it down for you. If you work on a job, run a business; go to school, or whatever you may do to earn a living, you give on average 40 to 50 hours a week to that duty. You give another 6 to 8 hours a night sleeping on average. You may have 1 to 2 hours of drive time a day in your commute back and forth and what you're left with is about 3 to 6 hours of me time plus whatever you have on your off days. That personal "me time" is usually what separates the stronger Christians from the weaker Christian, married or single.

A weaker Christian or carnal Christian tends to spend their "me time" doing the same things; worldly activities or things that non-followers of Christ engage in. The stronger Christian spends a major part of their "me time" on spiritual matters. You see if we both go to the same church, we both work the same type of job, and we both have the same size family what is separating us is our spiritual walk. Why is one person more carnally minded and one more spiritually minded? I guarantee you that the one who is more spiritually minded in their "me time" is reading and studying the Word, watching spiritual videos, reading spiritually based books and listening to spiritual music while the carnally minded is engaging in things like reality TV, carnal phone conversations, reading fictional books and much more. I'm not saying that any of that is sin, but the more of it you do cancels out the time that you could be spending on more spiritual matters. Remember you only have so much personal time in a day and what you choose to do with that time determines who you become, and the result is what you are when you get squeezed. I always say we're all like sponges in that whatever you dip a sponge in, it soaks it up and when you squeeze it, whatever it was dipped in is the only thing that will come out. During your personal "me time," are you dipping into the things of God or are you dipping into the things of society? When you are *squeezed* in life, we will see what comes out of you.

Let us talk about some of the, "me time" activities in which the single Christian should be engaged. I will not call this first one an activity really, but the single should have plenty of time to engage in helping spread the Gospel of Jesus Christ. The single Christians time should not be divided between relationships and family in the way that a married Christians would be. The single Christian should not have time to get in trouble with the opposite sex because they should not be alone dating or hanging out with the opposite sex for hours at a time. The single Christian should be mindful of spending late hours with the opposite sex at night even in the privacy of their home. I am saying this because you are totally setting yourself up to fall towards your fleshly desires as a single person if you engage in that type of activity. On the other hand, those things that pertain to dating, romance, sexual activity should be the focus of only the married Christian. The married Christian shouldn't spend all their "me time" the same way as a single. They should be dancing, eating, romancing, and making love along with the other spiritual acts of studying the Word, listening to spiritual music, Christian videos, and spreading the Gospel. This seems to be a mystery in today's times and if you look at it with an open mind you will see that it really makes sense. If you are single or even if you're a married person today and can think back to when you were single, it was those times when you should have been more focused on building your relationship with Christ. A Christ led relationship would have prevented the building of relationships that didn't lead to marriage, that ended up leaving you fragmented with pieces of your heart left carelessly here and there. If this was you before you said I do, you are now reaping some of what you sowed in those early years of FLAWED living and early relationships. Of course I'm not referring to you if you never entered a relationship before the one you said I do, but you would surely in today's time be one of the very few.

Married women, single women and Love

The final part of this passage is talking about the married woman versus the virgin woman. There is clearly a difference between a wife and a virgin, who is referred to as the woman not yet married. We must understand that God meant for the first time we made love to be the consummation of our marriage, so it was God's original intent for the married and non-married to have a slightly different kind of lifestyle. The Bible talks about three types of women; 1) It talks about a wife, 2) Widow and 3) a Virgin. Today we only usually talk about two types of women; single and married. I believe if we get back to calling youngsters virgins and not single, maybe they will have a better chance at staying virgins until they say I do. A virgin should not have the same urges or temptations of a wife because her time belongs to the Lord. I know that sounds foreign because it is hard to find a virgin over the age of 18. You can't really think that you can watch and listen to the same sensual things that a married couple does and not rustle up the urges a married couple has. You definitely can't taste the sweet nectar of love making and not have those desires. One of the problems with all the technology of today is that you get to see and hear things that ultimately become temptations that drive you to the sins of the flesh. The lust of the eyes, the lust of the flesh and the pride of life will always lead you to a life of sin. God advises us through His Word to love not the world or the things of the world, because if you do, the love of the Father is not in you. With that said if you are single, dedicate your time, energy, and efforts to the Lord, until you say I do. If you are married, you must divide that time with the Lord and your spouse. The time you do choose to devote to your spouse, you should learn to make good use of that time. Spending this time together will ultimately seal the destiny of your marriage union. When I say seal the destiny, I literally mean that spending time together will determine if your marriage is one of just barely making it, up and down like a roller coaster, or flourishing like the Love Byrd's. We have come to discover that when you spend time with someone, you create opportunities to increase the loving feelings or lose the loving feelings. I know that true Agape love is not a feeling but a choice. However, there are other meanings to the word love and that is where most of you are living. I have decided that since that is where most of you are living I might as well come and visit your neighborhood while I'm writing this book. Most couples today survive or thrive based on feelings and if that is where you have decided to stay, I have some advice that will help you in your journey. I am not saying that this is the best way, because God's Agape love, forgiveness, grace, and mercy are the best way. My wife always says that she loves me and whenever anyone asks her why she loves me she says "For no reason." She says that because if you have a reason you create a condition and with a condition, you create expectations and with expectations, you create the potential for the demise of a relationship because most of us can't match the expectations put on us by our spouse. With that said, you must learn how to spend quality time with your spouse to sustain a flourishing marriage. That sounds like some of the lamest advice you've ever heard I know, but most couples don't know how to really have quality time in their marriage. They may have had quality time when they were dating, but soon after the honeymoon quality time became just time.

I would define quality time as time spent where the both of you are doing things that you enjoy together. That doesn't mean doing things that one of you enjoys and the other dislikes, or one of you enjoys and the other tolerates. For it to be quality time, both of you have to enjoy the time spent together. Anything else is just time spent and in the grand scheme of feelings driven marriage, it is actually a step in the wrong direction. Some people think that time spent in a marriage is good no matter what you are doing, but I beg to differ. You see if I spend time with my wife and I don't enjoy that time, and on the other hand I spend time with someone else and I have a great time, I have just grown closer to the person I enjoyed spending time with than my spouse. If I want to have a flourishing marriage, I should enjoy spending time with my wife more than I enjoy spending time with anyone else. Unfortunately, most couples never see that side of marriage. They experience it during their courtship, but most never ever see it again, once they say I do. Subsequently, most married couples end up losing that loving feeling before they reach year two of their marriage.

Chapter 7
If It Doesn't Fit, You Must Get Rid of It

^{14} Don't be tied up as equal partners with people who don't believe. What does righteousness share with that which is outside the Law? What relationship does light have with darkness? ^{15} What harmony does Christ have with Satan? What does a believer have in common with someone who doesn't believe?^{16} What agreement can there be between God's temple and idols? Because, we are the temple of the living God, just as God said, I live with them, and I will move among them. I will be their God,

and they will be my people. 2 Corinthians 6:14-16 Common English Bible (CEB).

Most people that have worshipped in the church or studied the Bible for any length of time have heard about this passage of Scripture. This Scripture is clear that believers and non-believers should not join in marriage or in major fellowship. What seems to leave a doorway for your own judgment is a relationship between two people that are both believers but they are at different stages and levels of their commitment to Christ. What happens in relationships is instead of people adhering to the equally yoked principle; they often try to see what other things they have in common that would override the fact that they are not joint believers when it comes to their spiritual walk. Therefore, they try to use the things they do have in common to try to circumvent this Biblical truth when it comes to relationships. The problem with that is; God is smarter than man is. God's ways are flawless while man's ways are flawed. God sees the big picture whereas man usually has tunnel vision and makes short-term decisions with long-term manifestations. Many couples that attempt to choose a mate use the same interests (sports, movies, board games, and food) to choose a person versus how committed they are to their faith and belief system in Christ. They discover later on, that there is eventually no way of getting around the spiritual side of a person. The differences of a believer and non-believer or the differences of a committed believer and a casual or carnal believer always come back to haunt a relationship. That relationship ultimately ends in one of just a few scenarios. Typically, the non-believer drains the entire desire to follow God out of the believer and apostasy sets in for the believer. They slowly and gradually fall away from serving God faithfully, because when two people spend that kind of time together something is going to change. For example, a wife that goes to church on a regular basis may become embarrassed because everyone knows she's married but they never or hardly ever see her husband at church with her. The truth is most people are not as concerned with you and your situation as you think they are, but it feels like that to you because you feel that way on the inside. We see a lot of this in our marriage counseling and usually it's the case of a Christian woman settling for her emotions over God's clear instructions or either being fooled by someone telling you they are believers of God but never really show Godly attributes. Again, this is where you see the love is blind syndrome. These situations usually end up in a marriage that after the passion goes away, and she opens her eyes, she realizes she needs God in her life and at this time he's just not interested and he no longer plays the game. You're married now and he feels like you have to take him like he is. At this stage in a marriage, it starts to wear on the relationship and ultimately wears on your relationship with God. The woman wonders will God ever meet her prayers concerning her husband, totally forgetting that this was the choice she made going against God's Word about being equally yoked.

This is what God has always been trying to save His family from which is anything that will ultimately separate you from Him. Even if a woman stays with God, and with a man who is not totally committed to Christ, the potential is that without involvement in spiritual things from dad, the children most likely will not follow Christ.

Why sure there have been occasions where the believer has won over the non-believer, but that is a rarity and not usually the case. Even in those cases, it's usually a long battle and a lot of marital misuse and abuse along the way. We know women personally that are still fighting that battle even after 20 years of believing God and trying all they can to win their husband to Christ. The husbands are not bad guys, and many have accepted Jesus as Lord, but they don't want to get involved in the whole church thing with their wives. Women ultimately get lonely at church without their husband when everyone knows they are married. In some cases, this has led to the woman losing some of her fervor for the things of God and that is again, what God is trying to protect us from. I know you may have felt as if that was the person for you, and you might have even felt like the nice ones were not in the church, but Ishmael will never be God's best. If you don't know that story you can check it out in Genesis Chapter 16. You can try to do God's business your own way or you can give in and do it His way. His way is flawless and your ways have flaws. I recall a young lady who experienced this Scripture in a very tough way. She went through a whirlwind romance and fell for a guy from overseas, and tasted the forbidden fruit of sex before marriage. The biggest problem with this relationship ended up being the child that was born out of wedlock and the ensuing break up and battle of raising the baby. You see, the lady wanted to raise her baby as a Christian and enjoy holidays such as Christmas and Resurrection Sunday, but she soon found out the father of the child grew up as a Muslim and wanted no part of Christianity for the child. This of course ended the relationship between the two of them but this only started a custody battle over the child that would probably go on for the next 18 years. By now, this should be ringing in your ears when I say this is what God was trying to protect us from. This is amazing to us when we hear this Scripture, we don't often take it as God speaking to us but rather we take it as a preacher or parent trying to keep us from enjoying a good relationship. Not only are the preachers and the parents trying to help us but also God is showing His love for us by trying to protect our future relationship with Him. This should also be seen as God crying out to us for a relationship with us and our families. God doesn't want anything or anybody to come between that. He knows that being yoked up equally will bring us closer to Him and instead of further apart as the unequally yoked relationship tends to do.

Chapter 8
Sleeping With the Enemy

²⁶ Be angry without sinning. Don't let the sun set on your anger. ²⁷ Don't provide an opportunity for the devil. Ephesians 4:26, 27 Common English Bible (CEB)

Within this chapter, we are using this short passage of Scripture to demonstrate that God's principles always work. I would be lying to you if I told you to never get angry or that you will never get angry with your spouse. I won't say that it's impossible to avoid anger but actually it's improbable that you will avoid it. Anger is a real emotion and there is nothing wrong with it as long as we do the right thing with it. When we allow our anger to lead us into poor decision-making, our marriages are doomed to fail. However, if we deal with it wisely and make proper decisions, anger can be a positive emotion. Anger will alert you that there is something either wrong with you or wrong with the situation you are facing. Anger can be a protective mode at someone coming against your spouse or children. Therefore, you see, anger is not always the issue, but the sin that can often follow anger is the problem. If prayer and rational decision-making follow your anger, you will make the best of this emotion but in most situations, it is followed with irrational decisions, which lead to unwanted consequences. Your anger then will get the best of you and put those close to you at risk.

The most dangerous thing you can do with anger is to go to bed and sleep with it. Let us just pretend that anger is a person; well I am here to let you know that "she" doesn't make a good bed fellow. When you are angry and you do not deal with it properly, you will only make things worse. I have heard it described by Pastor Jimmy Evans; if you walked by a house with beautiful green grass, every day drop a small dose of yard killer on the grass to poison it, eventually that poison if not dealt with will spread and eat away at that entire yard. Anger towards your spouse if not dealt with will turn to un-forgiveness. Always remember, un-forgiveness is like drinking poison and expecting the other person to die. Un-forgiveness will always be more damaging to the one who is holding on to it while the other person is going about their business. It will cause the person holding on to un-forgiveness to slowly die inside. Not all anger comes from a bad place. Often, misunderstandings lead to this kind of anger, which can lead to un-forgiveness, bitterness, and wrath. For example, a wife could have taken something her husband said the wrong way or even heard it the wrong way and if she doesn't confront it properly, the misunderstanding can be internalized and she may allow it to turn into anger and eventually poison; all over something he doesn't even know he did or said. This is not just something that can happen to a wife but a husband can do the same thing. The spouse that seeks peace over conflict often does this. If a spouse decides to discuss the situation, one of the two may desire to avoid the discussion all together. Avoiding the discussion will cause the day to be better. When a couple knowingly avoids a discussion, anger could grow inside of them. As the anger continues to build, one innocent push of the wrong button could cause a huge ***BOOM***. After the huge explosion, comes the rage, which may catch your spouse off guard.

Have you ever heard your spouse say, "Where did all of this come from?" That was probably your signal that you had some pint-up frustration and un-forgiveness. Another point is to consider is if you haven't discussed the issue between each other to get clarity or even an apology. This is why forgiveness and good communication are essential elements of a successful marriage. I once remember a time where my wife and I were so upset with each other over an incident that occurred at the church of all places. When the incident occurred, we both thought that the other had lost their mind. After all we had been through together, and all we were facing with the call of God on our lives, how could he/she act like this? I could not believe that after we both confessed our sides of the story to a third party, it came out that both of us were not seeing and hearing all of the same information. Our reactions were based on what each other had heard which, was understandable. Once we knew what the missing piece of information was, it all made sense. The sad thing about it was that it was all just a misunderstanding. However, there was still poison inside of both of us from past experience. This is one of the scary things about un-forgiveness. To not forgive someone can be hidden deep inside of us, and you don't realize it until a certain situation causes it to surface. So, if you are married, make it a habit to practice forgiveness. Also, include making a habit to calmly get to the source of any disagreement. The sooner you forgive your spouse the better for you, and the better it ultimately is for your marriage. Forgiveness is something many people struggle with, however please keep in mind that you have been forgiven for everything you've ever done, or will ever do by the sacrifice of Jesus on the Cross. With that in mind, how dare you not forgive your spouse for something they have done or said! There is nowhere in the Scriptures that allows to hold on to un-forgiveness. We always refer to the Jesus principle of forgiveness, which is seven times seventy in a day[i]. Although forgiveness is sometimes tough, it is always a decision. Do not think that your spouse has to do something to earn it, just decide to do it because Jesus commands you to. Like the Nike campaign said, "Just Do It."

Chapter 9
Whisper It, Submission

²¹ and submit to each other out of respect for Christ. ²² For example, wives should submit to their husbands as if to the Lord. ²³ A husband is the head of his wife like Christ is head of the church, that is, the savior of the body.²⁴ So wives submit to their husbands in everything like the church submits to Christ. ²⁵ As for husbands, love your wives just like Christ loved the church and gave himself for her. ²⁶ He did this to make her holy by washing her in a bath of water with the word. ²⁷ He did this to present himself with a splendid church, one without *any sort of stain or wrinkle on her clothes, but rather one that is holy and blameless. ^{28} That's how husbands ought to love their wives—in the same way as they do their own bodies. Anyone who loves his wife loves himself. ^{29} No one ever hates his own body, but feeds it and takes care of it just like Christ does for the church ^{30} because we are part of his body. ^{31} This is why a man will leave his father and mother and be united with his wife, and the two of them will be one body. ^{32} Marriage is a significant allegory, and I'm applying it to Christ and the church. ^{33} In any case, as for you individually, each one of you should love his wife as himself, and wives should respect their husbands.* Ephesians 5:21-33 Common English Bible (CEB).

Now you know I couldn't go and write a book on marriage from a Christian perspective and not talk about submission and authority. This passage is one of the most common talked about passages of Scripture as it relates to our roles, and it has a lot to say and a lot to be interpreted. Apostle

Paul was definitely using some high touch writing styles in Ephesians. Paul uses some interchangeable word choices in the above passage of Scripture; words like "submit and reverence;" "submit and love;" "wife and church"; "husband and Christ." You would need to do some literary interpretation to really understand what is going on with this text of Scripture. I will try to give you some of the nuggets that I found in here so that you'll really understand what he was telling us by inspiration of the Holy Spirit. Verse: 21 submitting yourselves, one to another in the fear of God is not recapping the beginning of the chapter, but it is a part of the statement to husbands and wives that would follow. This is a very important point and I don't want you to miss it. I say that because most translations of your Bible have a break and a sub-heading in between verse: 21 and verse: 22. If you want to verify this, you would have to look at the original writings to see that verse: 22 really said "Wives unto your own husbands as unto the Lord." This is critical because the only way you know he was talking about wives submitting themselves is because verse: 21 had just told you. Listen as you read verse: 22 without Verse: 21"Wives unto your own husbands as unto the Lord." If you walked up to a group of wives and said that statement, their response to you would probably be "WHAT?" The translators wanted to make sure wives knew what he was talking about so they added it to verse: 22. With that established Paul immediately explained what he meant by submitting one to another. The wives submission starting at verse: 22 and the husband's submission starting at verse: 25. It goes a little something like this. Submit yourselves to one another. Wives should do it like you would unto the Lord because your husband is to you like Christ is to the church. Husbands your submission is expressed as love. The kind of love expressed as Christ expressed to the church. Here is another way to look at it. Our Lord is the Head of the Church and the husband is head of the wife; however, our Lord died to redeem the church and so should the husband be willing to die for his wife and children.

Not necessarily a physical death, but to die to your own ways and desires for the sake of treating her/them the way God would desire for you to. I can hear all of the women saying "Amen, now that's what we're talking about." Not only are many husbands not willing to die physically for their wives but many husbands are not even willing to give up the remote control, the golf clubs, basketball, video games or even re-runs of sports center on ESPN. It's amazing that men expect their wives to give things up for them or the family but selfishly they wouldn't think of it. If we would all just see submission and authority, the way it was meant to be seen, most marital problems would suddenly be over. The world would automatically want to do it our way and our society as we know it would be forever changed to represent God's love on the earth. This is the power, which has great potential when the love of Christ is displayed in a marriage. Everyone is chasing love. We know the chase ends up in many different formats, but the underlying truth is we all want it and need it. We were created in the image of God and we were created to express love to God in addition to one another. When God's man/woman doesn't express God's love in the earth and in marriage, the mess that we see today is the result.

I would like to share with you some of a letter a man wrote after he was recently divorced. The message in this letter may inspire you to change, if not, I'm not sure what will. What I'm getting ready to share with you are 20 wise marriage tips from a divorced man. You'll have to purchase his book to get his advice completely, but I will give you the introduction to what he has learned. You wouldn't normally think that a divorced man would give good advice on being a husband, but this man had definitely been through some serious hardship and now he knows that marriage is worth fighting for. He is speaking out of tremendous loss and pain, and I think we would be wise to learn these things before it's too late as was the case for him. The title of his writings is;

Marriage **Advice I Wish I Would Have Had**, Gerald Rogers, Author of "You have one Life to Live; Live Big" [3]

> **1) Never stop courting**. Whatever you did to get her is what you need to do to keep her. If you put the 3 words, to get her a little closer you'll see they make one great word; together. That is what continuing to date, pursue, and chase after one another will do for your marriage. It will keep you together. It almost amazes me how everyone has heard this and seemingly knows that this principle will work, but a great percentage of couples that I have ever known, talked to or counseled; don't practice it on a regular basis. Without it, subtle separation creeps in and before you know it, distance and

---

[3] Gerald Rogers, You have one Life to Live, Live Big, accessed September 26, 2014, http://geraldrogers.com/marriage-advice-i-wish-i-would-have-had/

disconnection is all over you and you do not know what to do about it.

2) Protect Your Own Heart. When he advises you to protect your own heart, it is not talking about protecting it from your spouse. You should actually protect your heart from everyone else other than your spouse. No one should be allowed to enter the space that was once set aside for your spouse. You should protect your heart with lock and key. Your spouse should be the only person with the combination to that special place. I know you want to give your heart to your children, but they should have a different place away from that special place reserved for your spouse. If you do this, you will not experience the distance and separation that many experience. There is a serious flaw in many marriages as it relates to the place you give your children. The moment your kids get first place and you relegate your spouse to second place it is the beginning of major separation. If you haven't had children yet, you may not believe what I am saying but trust me, I know what I am talking about.

3) **<u>Fall in Love OVER and OVER and OVER again</u>**. Falling in love is only good advice when it includes repetition for life. Without that repetition, falling in love is only a precursor to falling out of love. Amazingly, the falling out of love hurts more than the falling in love feels good. Reason being is that the falling out of love happens second and it is the more recent memory. The falling out of love usually lasts longer than the falling in love did. I am not against the feelings of love or infatuation, but they are not enough to base a relationship on in and of themselves. Falling in love over and over again really goes back to doing what you did to get her

in order to keep her. The same holds true for the female. Whatever interest you showed in him and whatever honor and respect you bestowed on him, must continue throughout the relationship.

4) <u>Always see the best in her</u>. This goes back to the popular 80/20 rule. People in marriages tend after a while to focus on the 20 percent they do not like about their spouse rather than the 80 percent they do like. It is human nature that after being around someone closely for an extended period you tend to become bothered by his or her quirks. The things that you have in common just become unnoticed and the differences start to surface. Your thought life begins to be bombarded with negativity. That is why the Bible urges us to guard our thoughts with everything within us. If you are able to keep the negative thoughts to a minimum and cover them with a multitude of positive thoughts, you will always see the best in each other.

5) It's Not Your Job To Change Or Fix Her. You do not marry someone to fix them. You do play a vital role in influencing change, but change nonetheless is their choice. Love your spouse unconditionally and allow the word of God to be the change agent in both of your lives. Renewing your mind daily from God's Word is the safest place to change and fix yourself. The moment you focus on trying to change something about your spouse is the moment they will feel rejection and usually either shut down or fight back. You don't want either of those outcomes in your relationship. Be O.K. with who they are and love them unconditionally.

6) Take Full Accountability For Your Own Emotions. We often try to blame our negative emotions on something that has happened to us. This is especially true of husbands and wives. You are given free will by God, with which you always have an option to choose life or death in a given situation. It is immature to choose to respond negatively when you feel you were wronged. I know it is the easiest and most natural thing to do; nevertheless, it is not the mature thing to do. Forgiveness and humility will allow you more often than not to make the life decision in cases of conflict with your spouse.

7) <u>Never Blame Your Wife If You Get Frustrated Or Angry With Her</u>. Your reaction is only because it is triggering something inside of YOU. We all have a history and a past that causes us to respond the way we do. Unless we get in touch with our own personal issues, walls, triggers or coping mechanisms, we will continue to be moved by the actions of others. We also have to mature in love. It is really a sign of spiritual immaturity to argue with someone. There may be times when a sensible debate is necessary but you can't be so dogmatic that you think someone else has to surrender their will to yours. Some of us do not even surrender our wills to God and He doesn't force us. He gives us the opportunity to surrender our will to Him, and the rest is a decision that we have to make. In all we do or say, there is always a choice. We can choose to get upset and become extremely angry, or we can choose to remain calm. Life and death is in the power of your tongue; choose life like decisions.

8) Don't Run Away When She's Upset. Men, I know it is hard to deal with your wife when she is upset, but space is not usually, what she wants. That is usually what you want when you're upset. What she wants is for you to understand her. Understand how she feels. Don't focus so much on the words that she is saying, rather get in touch with the feelings of her heart. If you run away when she is upset, she will often times feel abandonment and that is not the signal you want to send.

9) Be Silly. Remember laughter does you good. It is compared to medicine for your body in the Bible. If you don't have fun and laugh, the connection in your marriage will dry up like a cactus in the desert.

10) Fill Her Soul Everyday. It is our nature to desire for others to fill our needs on a daily basis. It starts with our parents as a child. However, when it comes to marriage we should be focusing on filling the needs, wants and desires of our spouse. If we do this on a daily basis, we will eliminate most of the marital problems today.

11) Be Present. If there is one thing that is so very common in marriage as it relates to men, it's this one thing right here. Men learn after a while to be present in body but absent in the mind. We learn to have conversations with our wives that we later have no idea of what was said. How is this? It's almost like when you drive home from work unconsciously. I can't tell you how many times I've pulled up to my driveway and I don't remember the drive home at all. I've done the drive so many times that I can do it with my subconscious. That may be O.K. with driving home from work, but it is never O.K. when it comes to being with your wife.

12) Be Willing To Take Her Sexually. This should be a natural thing when you are in love with someone. There are factors today that have made this more difficult for many men. Men being the visual creatures that we are have so many distractions facing us sexually. Everywhere you look, sex is being put in our face. Pornography availability and consumption is at an all-time high. Commercials on television are full of sexually tempting women. If you are not careful, your wife will not satisfy you because of lust creeping in to your heart. I have made it a habit to make sure my glance doesn't linger on women that are physically attractive to me. I am human, so I do notice them, but I don't let it go too far. I don't watch things pertaining to sex or half naked women on television. I am protecting my passion and myself for my wife. I want my eyes and heart to always be for my bride. I can absolutely say that after 23 years of marriage, my wife still does it for me, just as she did when we said "I Do."

13) <u>Don't Be An Idiot</u>. There are many times that we do things to each other in our marriage that we know are way out of line. That is how a child acts when he/she is so upset that they don't know what else to do. This is no way for an adult to act. This is no way for someone to act towards someone that they love. Loving your spouse is the key to not being an idiot.

14) <u>Give Her Space</u>. Women can often find themselves lost in the whirlwind of family. They can give themselves over to you and the children as well as working outside of the home. You would be a wise man to give her opportunities to get away and recharge her batteries. Maybe an hour at the spa or even you taking the kids out for a couple of hours and letting her enjoy herself at home. Whatever you choose, make sure you give her time away from you and the kids. Most women don't require that much time. I have had women tell me, "If I could just get 1 hour a week that would be helpful." If you do this, she will be better for you and the children. Happy wife equals a happy life.

15) <u>Be Vulnerable</u>. Vulnerability is missing in most of the marriages if not all of the marriages that we counsel. Many couples do not trust each other with their deepest fears, hurts or pains. Often it is because they have done the wrong things with it in the past. The baggage that we bring in to marriage also plays a large role. As a man, if you would learn to be vulnerable with your spouse, you would see that your wife would connect to you more. It has not been portrayed as the thing to do if you're a man. Men don't share feelings according to the stereotype. I beg to differ with that train of thought. Men should share feelings with their wives and the marriage would be all the better for it.

16) Be Fully Transparent. I don't know of anyone that wants to be fully transparent even with themselves. You have to be taught that it is the best thing for your marriage. Not only is it the best thing for your marriage, it is also the best thing for you individually. Secrets will eat you up inside. Just think about it like this. If I'm always open and truthful, I won't have any problems remembering what I've told my spouse in the past. However, if I'm hiding things, I will have to try and remember what I told her in the past so that I can say the same thing in her presence. That is just too much work; when all I have to do is be transparent from the get go.

17) Never Stop Growing. This has been one of my wife and I's biggest secrets to success and unity in our marriage. From day one, we have always grown together. We read the same books. We share the same friends. We watch most of the same programs. We share activities. If she gets information that I don't have, she shares it with me and I do the same with her. It has created a "Oneness", which is so natural to us, that is obvious to all.

18) <u>Don't Worry About Money</u>. Money is often reported as one of the biggest causes for divorce. I look at money as a magnifier. Money will only allow you to be who you are. The more of it you have, the more you can show who you really are. During the times when we were barely making it we have been close and when we have had abundance we have still been just as close. Money is not the issue for most people. The real issue for most people is who they really are inside.

19) <u>Forgive Immediately</u>. We always teach Jesus' forgiveness model in marriage.

Forgiveness is a funny thing. Depending on how hurt you are by the offense, has a lot to do with how easy or difficult it will be to forgive. Some things hurt so deep that you try to forgive, but it just doesn't seem to happen. It is in those times that I believe forgiveness becomes a spiritual battle. You have to really humble yourself and compare yourself to Jesus who humbled himself by going to cross. When we think that we should not have been treated a certain way, we can often look to Jesus to lighten the load of what we thought was just too much. Forgiveness is also like poison. When you don't forgive someone you think it is hurting them. That is like taking poison and expecting it to kill someone else. You are only hurting yourself and your relationship. Let it go and move on to a new day.

20) <u>Always Choose Love</u>. ALWAYS CHOOSE LOVE! Love endures long and is patient and kind; love never is envious nor boils over with jealousy. Love is not boastful or vainglorious nor does it display itself haughtily. Love is not conceited, arrogant, or inflated with pride. Love is not rude and doesn't act unbecomingly. Love, the God kind of love, does not insist on its own way because it is not self-seeking, touchy or resentful. Love takes no account of the evil done to it. Love does not rejoice at injustice and unrighteousness, but rejoices when right and truth prevail. Love leaves one ready to believe the best of every person,, and will endure everything without weakening. If you didn't know, these are words from 1 Corinthians Chapter 13, often referred to as the love chapter. This kind of love never fails.

Gerald Rodgers ended it by saying if you find wisdom in his pain, share it to those young husbands whose hearts are still full of hope, and with those couples you know, who may have forgotten how to love. His hope is that he may reach one that was like him and perhaps spark something or awaken something in him that he can learn to be the man his wife has been waiting for. I am passing on his wishes as requested, but in order to really view it from his point of view versus my point of view; you will have to purchase his book. Further down in verse 31of Ephesians 5, we come to know that this is the reason a man should leave his father and mother and cleave to his wife. The mystery of marriage is being unfolded in Scripture, and you must be born again to operate in it and to understand it fully. If you are not born again read Romans 10:9-10 and make a public confession to your local church or to another believer. Now that you are born again you have what it takes on the inside of you to actually pull off this great relationship called marriage.

Chapter 10
80/20 Rule

⁸From now on, brothers and sisters, if anything is excellent and if anything is admirable, focus your thoughts on these things: all that is true, all that is holy, all that is just, all that is pure, all that is lovely, and all that is worthy of praise. Philippians 4:8 Common English Bible (CEB)

We're going to use the principle spelled out in this Scripture to help understand the famous 80/20 rule. If you are not familiar with the 80/20 rule, it says that 80% of what your spouse does is probably good and 20% you would probably like to see change. Most people focus or magnify the 20%, which leads to discontentment in their relationships. Instead of magnifying the 20% you would like to see changed, you should focus on the 80% of good they are doing. Now, this has proven to be successful in marriage but the Bible has something more successful than the 80/20 rule. We can call it the 100/00 rule. Think about only the things that are+; true, honorable, just, pure, lovely, commendable, excellent, and praise worthy.

When you think about those attributes regarding your spouse, you will "think yourself" from a floundering marriage into a flourishing marriage. Your thought life produces what you see around you. That is why you must first "think yourself" from one failure to success. This is one rule that is a no brainer and will work every time. Some of you may be thinking that if you don't address the 20%, it may never change. You are correct. The 20% may never change, but it just might. One thing that doesn't work towards that kind of change is constantly thinking on it or nagging your spouse about it. Yes, I know there are those of you who are probably so deep into a bad marriage, that all you can think about is the 20% or maybe even getting out of the marriage. I'm here to tell you that your heart always follows your *dominant* thoughts. I used the word *dominant* because people think that they can just sample something and get the full benefit of it but that is not the case in matters of the heart. You have to go all in, full board and then and only then will you see and feel the manifested benefits of thinking the right things. Just think about it for a second. Current thinking about the negative aspects of your spouse all the time have gotten you to the point of possibly wanting out or at the least wondering if the marriage will ever get better. That strategy is obviously not working well for you. There are things that are at hard work against thinking along the more positive ways of Philippians 4:8. Some of the more obvious are television, radio, music, movies and most of the people you talk to in society today. Wow, when you look at it that way, you're going to have to put a specific strategy and plan in place to overcome that which is at work against you. Your plan is going to have to be as dominant as the enemy's strategies against you. The enemy is not playing and most people are trying to win the war against him without a plan. For example, if I wandered into the territory of a major foe of the United States wearing a stars and stripes shirt, a USA ball cap, a President Obama button on the pocket, lost, without a gun, radio, or transportation how long do you think I would last? I would probably be captured and tortured within a matter of minutes. This is what's happening with most of you on a daily basis in society and in your marriage. The enemy is torturing you in your marriage. The enemy's influence is so subtle that most of us don't even recognize it. Everywhere we go, we hear about how bad marriages are and how so many are ending up in divorce. Think about it, if you keep hearing negative news, it's going to frame the way we think in society. Either it will cause us to avoid marriage or it will cause us to take the easy road out if the marriage goes through a rough patch. This is one of the ways I believe the enemy is subtly duping our society as it relates to Godly marriages. Research is now recognizing where the phenomenon of the 50% divorce rate statistics were birthed[ii]. Reportedly, there are between 850,000 to 1,000,000 divorces a year and between 2,000,000 to 2,250,000 marriages a year in the United States.[iii] That would appear to be somewhere between a 40 to 50% divorce rate. However, we don't know how many of the new divorces are of the new marriages, especially when the average marriage lasts about 19 years. Studies that are more recent say the actual divorce rate of first time marriages is about 30% with 70%[iv] succeeding until the death of their spouse. It is the 30% that divorce and those that marry again after the death of a spouse that lead to the higher divorce rates because 2nd and 3rd marriages end up in a divorce at a much higher rate than first time marriages[v]. Therefore, when you hear negative statistics and you take into account the decline in how seriously we serve God and obey the Bible these days, it stands to reason that there will be a framing of the minds towards the decay of marriage. Back in the 1960s, 70% of adults in our country were traditionally married and by the early 2000s, that number was down to 50%[vi]. If you can understand that a man and a woman serving God, and following his rules in the Holy Bible, have a 75-80% success rate in marriage today, you will know that you can truly succeed in marriage today if you do it God's way.

I have just given you a plan along with the 100/00 rule, which will be the equivalent of you taking that same trip into enemy territory. This time you're a champion fighter pilot in a stealth bomber, with a fleet of other bombers beside, behind and in front of you. Where you were captured within minutes in the first scenario, I believe in this second scenario you'll be o.k.

Chapter 11
No "I" in Team

¹ Therefore, if there is any encouragement in Christ, any comfort in love, any sharing in the Spirit, any sympathy, ² complete my joy by thinking the same way, having the same love, being united, and agreeing with each other. ³ Don't do anything for selfish purposes, but with humility think of others as better than yourselves. ⁴ Instead of each person watching out for their own good, watch out for what is better for others.⁵ Adopt the attitude that was in Christ Jesus. Philippians 2:1-5 Common English Bible (CEB)

These five verses of Scripture are a brief overview and reminder of how God expects His family to operate in the earth. The Scriptures also demonstrate how Christ came to earth with a flawless plan to win a lost world. If our families would operate in these instructions of the Lord, the world would want what we have instead of the church wanting what the world has. What should be happening to win the world to Jesus is an overwhelming display of love in the marriages and families of believers. With that kind of love, the world would stop focusing on money, cars, clothes and homes and they would run after the Jesus we serve that gives us the ability to love the way we do. Instead, what you see is no difference in the marriages and families of most believers, so instead of the world chasing us for our love, we are chasing after the world for its lust of material things. Some kind of a way, someone is going to have to initiate a love movement that is so drastic that it gets the attention of even the hard-core sinner who is loaded with money but also loaded with loneliness at night.

This is amazing how much in life you can apply this passage of Scripture. I know we are going to apply it to marriage and we can see that it was applied to Jesus and how he operated in the earth realm. I even applied this passage of Scripture once as a strategy for use by my son's AAU basketball team. I saw a group of individuals that played more for themselves than for the team or for each other. I gave my son this passage and told him to pass it on to his teammates, with the understanding that if they would simply apply these principles they would have fun and become more successful as a unit. I was not shocked at all with the operating of these principles because they had great success. When they reverted to the old selfish nature, they under-performed. The same truth applies to your marriage and family. You can look at your marriage as a team; and if the team is operating as a bunch of individuals versus operating as a single unit, the team will be less successful. Then it will under-perform. When the leaders of the team; the husband and the wife, work together and prefer each other, it gives the team such an advantage over other teams that operate individually. Teamwork from the leaders of the family will also spill over to the rest of the troops. The children learn by what they see their leaders perform. Leadership that tells them to do one thing yet does another has duped many a child. Those types of leaders are foolish to believe that the children will not do what they see. Newsflash, your children will learn more by what they see than by what you say. Since this is a principle that holds true, it would make more sense for you and your spouse as the leaders of your team to get on the same page in every area of your marriage.

Finances are a big area in marriage where leaders need to get on the same page. We counsel many couples that simply don't trust one another in the area of finances. Many couples that have a two income families pay their bills separately. They have separate bank accounts. He might be paying the rent and the car payment, while she is paying the utilities and the groceries. He doesn't know what she makes or anything about her banking account and she doesn't know what he makes or information about his account. Both the husband and wife know that the way they are operating is not a God flawless plan. The couple may realize that the way they operate financially is FLAWED; however, they just do not trust one another to do the right thing. There is no unity in this type of arrangement and the root behind it is usually a lack of trust. The lack of trust may stem from previous mistakes, or something from a previous relationship.

Still another FLAWED area we see is in child rearing. A lot of it has to do with the number of increasing blended families and some of it may be from the way the husband and wife were raised by their parents. Most couples do not plan ahead of time how they will handle tough issues in child rearing. Most couples simply tackle issues as they arise and this is one of the most FLAWED ways to be overwhelmed by problems with the children.

What about hobbies? Hobbies are another area that can divide a marriage without even knowing how it is happening. Hobbies can be the silent killer to a marriage. If the husband is involved in hobbies he enjoys while the wife is involved in other hobbies that she enjoys, what you will eventually see is two people who love to do things apart from one another. Now if that does not represent a FLAWED system I don't know what does. The worst thing that can happen in this type of marriage is if the hobbies by one of them involve someone of the opposite sex. That is a recipe for infidelity. The number one person of the opposite sex that you should be enjoying a hobby with is your spouse. All of these area's I have discussed and more need the team play strategies described earlier. This passage of Scripture is a recipe for unity in any marriage and more importantly, it should be the recipe for flawless unity in your marriage.

Chapter 12
Remove That 2 x 4

^{1}"Don't judge, so that you won't be judged. ^{2} You'll receive the same judgment you give. Whatever you deal out will be dealt out to you. ^{3} Why do you see the splinter that's in your brother's or sister's eye, but don't notice the log in your own eye? ^{4} How can you say to your brother or sister, 'Let me take the splinter out of your eye,' when there's a log in your eye? ^{5} You deceive yourself! First take the log out of your eye, and then you'll see clearly to take the splinter out of your brother's or sister's eye. Matthew 7:1-5 Common English Bible (CEB)

I don't think we would be distorting the text if we inserted the word "spouse" here in place of brother. If you are born again and your spouse is born again, then they are also your brother or sister in Christ. We know that it was not talking about your blood brother, and it was not just talking about males, so let's insert spouse in place of brother, and look how easily you could apply this passage to your marriage. *And how do you look at the speck in your spouse's eye but do not consider the plank from your own eye, Hypocrite! First remove the plank from your own eye and then you will see clearly to remove the speck from your spouse's eye.* Now doesn't that sound like something you can and should apply to our marriage? If I read this to most of society, they would probably assume that it was actually in the Bible. Although it is not written in Scripture this way, this would be a good way for married couples to look at more Scriptures. We don't want to just get in the habit of treating a fellow Christian in a Biblical way without treating our own spouse in that same way or even better. I am telling you from experience, if you ever learn to get this within your spirit to where it automatically comes up when you get squeezed, you will come out of disagreements so much faster than you ever have in the past. Eventually, you will even start to totally change the approach or the way you handle your spouse, which will lead to less arguments.

You must admit, there is something inside of you that makes you want to be right all the time, even when you are wrong. There are voices that will speak to you and twist a lie into some version of truth. You are going to have to purposely, resist the temptation to give in and respond to your spouse using that voice. You may hear it and you may respond to it but your response must be to run far from it as fast as you can. Sometimes it seems as if that voice screams at you loudly while the voice of the Holy Spirit whispers quietly in the background. Yet, you must obey the still quiet voice of the Holy Spirit and look at yourself. Look at what you could have done or said differently before you criticize or correct your spouse. I'm not saying that your criticism or correction wouldn't have been well warranted, but maybe your plank is how you're saying it or when you're saying it. Does it flow off your tongue like honey or is it coming off bitter and sour? When differences arise, let the Holy Spirit first deal with the plank in your eye, and once you've removed that 2x4, you may be able to see more clearly. Just for a moment, hold something as thick as a 2x4 board in front of one of your eyes. You may even be able to use one of your own arms as the board. Hold your arm in front of one of your eyes and then try to see things as clearly with the same range as you were able to before. You cannot do it. Yes, you can still see, but your range is limited and whichever eye is covered, leaves you vulnerable on that side. With this example, you can see what the Scriptures are saying in the above passage. You may be missing something if you rush to judgment. You may very well need to admit to yourself "I've possibly missed something due to limited peripheral vision." It is amazing sometimes how your perception of a situation changes if you point the finger at yourself, instead of at your spouse. I can remember a time feeling totally disrespected by my wife, and nothing she or anyone else could say would make me see it any other way. That was the case, until I was able to look at possible ways that I could have handled the situation differently. I also had to look at the record of accomplishment of my wife and knowing who she was. After looking at things differently (removing the plank from my eye), I was able to see that there was no disrespect intended by my wife, and she didn't even know that what she had said or did was disrespectful. The great thing about dealing with yourself is that your spouse will usually do the same thing and instead of being at odds with each other, you both are forgiving and understanding of each other. Making these types of changes will not be easy and won't come without a battle. As I said earlier, you will be challenged by the voices in your head, which are part of Team You. These voices cheer for you; the voices also plead for you. The voices say everything you want to hear and the voices are familiar to you. With the voices speaking, it is time for you to put your team on the bench and put team Jesus into the game. The more you practice removing the plank in your own eye the easier it will get. Just like anything else in your life, if you want to change the way you operate, you will have to first change the way you think. In order to change the way you think, you are going to have to change your intake. Your intake is what you read, watch, and listen to. Clean your intake valve and you'll be able to renew your mind. This intake has been the problem of all problems. You know our saying is "God's way is flawless, and man's ways are flawed," and it is the lack of doing things God's way that creates problems in society. Marriage is no different. Without God's way, we create marital problems in society. We can easily parallel the problems in a marriage to the problems in our walk with Christ. The more you saturate yourself with the Word of God, spend time in His presence and do what His Word tells you to do, the fewer the marital problems you'll have. The Bible tells us to study and to show ourselves approved unto God. If that principle will work for studying the Bible, the Word of God will also work for our marriages. If you want to have a flourishing marriage, study the subject of marriage. I applaud you for taking the time to read this book.

This book is an opportunity for you to study the subject of marriage, which is one of the most important subjects in which you should be well informed. Keep thinking about all of the principles you have learned about marriage before your eyes. Please remember to remove that plank from your own eye so you can see to assist your spouse with the toothpick in their eye.

Chapter 13
Choose Them

¹Therefore, if there is any encouragement in Christ, any comfort in love, any sharing in the Spirit, any sympathy, ² complete my joy by thinking the same way, having the same love, being united, and agreeing with each other.³ Don't do anything for selfish purposes, but with humility think of others as better than yourselves. ⁴ Instead of each person watching out for their own good, watch out for what is better for others. Philippians 2:1-4 Common English Bible (CEB)

Now as it relates to your marriage, this could be one of the toughest things to do on a regular basis. From an equal standpoint, everyone has interests of his or her own and that is not a bad thing. There may be a problem if you place your interests over those of your spouse. I am not talking about the "door mat" types who do everything their spouse wants them to do because they are afraid to rock the boat. That is foolishness and a recipe for a bad marriage. You are taking the Scripture a bit too far in the other direction. You see, it cannot be a very bad thing to have interests of your own nor is it a bad thing that you look out for your own interests. If that were the case verse four wouldn't read the way it does. Verse four does not say that we are not to look out for our own interests at all; the intent is that we don't look out for our interest alone. Here is another way to look at it. Who is your father? If Satan is your father, you will act like him. You will be selfish and self-centered. If God is your father, you should be selfless and you should be a giver. You will have the best interest of your spouse at the forefront of your mind. If you feel yourself gravitating to the old nature of Satan, and you know you are born again, spend some time with God, your Father, until your thoughts and ways begin to change from the old nature to your new nature.

Depending on how long you have been in the old nature, will give you an indication on how much time and effort you are going to have to devote to getting to the other side. If your actions are on Satan's side, you are going to have to run this race in a way as to catch up first and then you can get over to God's side. This is going to take the renewing of your mind, which comes about by changing what you put in your head. You have to change what you've been listening to. Everyone should understand this key point. God is love and the only way to operate in love with your spouse is to operate the way God operates. When you find yourself making the wrong choices in marriage, start acting like Father God and you'll start choosing or preferring your spouse.

I can remember a time in my marriage where all I really wanted to do was play golf. I played so much golf that I even made myself believe that if I kept playing, I could one day reach either the PGA or the Seniors Tour as a professional. This was absurd because I wasn't even close to being a scratch golfer. I can remember being at work in the summers and leaving for lunch to go to the driving range to hit a bucket of balls, or thinking about taking the rest of the day off to play a round before heading home from work. I did not know it at the time but golf literally consumed my mind. I would hit whiffle balls up against my house leaving divots in the grass. I would watch every golf show on cable television as if the teachers were my very own instructors. I would get out of church and head straight for my golfing buddies and talk about when the next time we could get out to play. If that wasn't enough the thoughts of golf would creep into my prayers and distract me. Sure, I know there are far worse things a husband could be doing, but the point here was that golf consumed me to the point of selfishness and self-centeredness. The Godly thing to do would have been to spend more time with my wife working on my marriage and spending more time in the Word of God to find out what God wanted me to do with this one life He gave me to live. Your thing might not be golf, it might be fishing, shopping, television, or knitting; whatever it is. If it takes away time from God and time from your mate, you are probably way too involved in it and your marriage will suffer. I am not saying that your marriage is in trouble. But, during the time I was consumed by golf I had a good marriage, but in retrospect, it was no way near what it has become now, by giving up a self-centered activity for the priority of my marriage. One thing I do not know is if I had kept up my self-centered addiction, would I have ever reached the potential in my marriage that I have today. I feel confident to say that I would not have and I would not be giving to the world what I am giving to it today. I would not have been doing with the one life I have to live what God had intended for me to do with it. Sure, I was born again and on my way to heaven. But how many other people was I helping along the way to get there. I was on God's team but I was playing selfishly. I was literally riding the bench. Now I am a vital player on God's team and it feels so much better to be off the bench and in the action. Can you imagine what the effect would be in the world if every marriage took on the attributes of Philippians 2:3-4? We would have instant success in our marriages and we could instantly paint a picture for our children that would have them desire the same thing. You would take away most if not all of the problems in marriage and it would create such a desire for the world to want to do marriage God's way. No longer would men need to be with men or women with women because what they seek is in a Godly marriage.

The hurts and pains that children view early in life may produce scars in the future. Such abuse should stop so that we can develop healthy children to grow into healthy adults. Oh what a beautiful thing this would be! Do not make this a fairy tale or a way out their dream, but make this a reality. This starts with you and it starts with me. One couple at a time and one family at a time; you have heard the slogan each one reach one or each one teach one. We can change this world and when asked how we did it, we can lead them to our God. We can direct them to our Bible and we can direct them to our Savior. Can you see it? Start by envisioning it in you and in your marriage. Once you are able to see the affect it has on your marriage, you will be able to see the whole world being influenced. I caution you, the enemy will try to fight you but be at peace, because you have power over him and over his devices against you. This type of love in action will defeat him every time. You will win. We will win. Marriage by God's design will win.

Chapter 14
Wow, Where Art Thou?

Wow, Where art thou?

³ Likewise, tell the older women to be reverent in their behavior, teaching what is good, rather than being gossips or addicted to heavy drinking. ⁴ That way they can mentor young women to love their husbands and children, ⁵ and to be sensible, morally pure, working at home, kind and submissive to their own husbands, so that God's word won't be ridiculed. Titus 2:3-5 Common English Bible (CEB)

This is obviously the plan set in place to get reproduction of Biblical women in the family of God. I think more than ever in times past, younger women needed to seek out Godly women, sit at their feet, and learn from them. I believe that a Godly woman also knows (or should know) the Word of God; this is so that she can instruct the younger women in Scripture. What she teaches will be on a sure foundation of the Word and not just something picked up in the world. For example, many older women will tell their daughters to keep a secret stash from their husbands in case something goes wrong in the marriage. I do not know of any book in the Bible that backs that up. The advice is based on fear that the relationship will not succeed or that the wife might need funds for a sudden emergency, (i.e. a man will mistreat their daughter). There would be less need for this type of instruction if they would instruct them on what type of man to marry and if their marriages would be a living example to them. This kind of worldly instruction is not biblically based. It is more like the mother that teaches her daughter to cut the butt off the ham before she puts it in the pan and in the oven. One day her daughter asks her why she cuts the butt off the ham and her mom doesn't know. Her mom says "I'll ask my mother." She asks her mom why she taught her to cut the butt off the ham. Her mother didn't know either; she said "That's the way my mom did it." "I'll ask your grandmother." Grandma tells her that the oven they had was too small to fit the entire ham so they had to cut it off to allow it to fit in the oven. The point of the story is, some things are passed down from generation to generation, but they are not necessarily Biblical truths and not necessarily needed today.

The less young women know about how to be a Biblically based woman and/or wife, the less they will be able to teach women, as they get older. If that cycle were to continue, we would end up with worldly women in the house of God. I really believe that there is a great opportunity and need for correct Biblical instruction to arise from women of

God to the young women of the church. There has been advancement with women in the world today as it relates to the work force and this is especially so in America. I believe if we look closer at the timeframe of these developments, we would see that not all of the advances have had a positive impact on society or family structures. I am not saying at this point we should go back to the days of old where women did not work outside of the home, but I am saying that more pressure needs to be put on the man to work and to allow the wife to be his helpmate. If you think I am trying to put too much pressure on the man, you should read your Bible. In addition, if you think the Bible puts a lot of pressure on the man you are correct. However, do not think for a second that a lot is not required of a woman as well.

Have you ever dug deeply into the Proverbs 31 woman? This woman was all that and a bag of chips as the saying goes. She ran the home and was a business woman also. I am not saying there is anything wrong with the advancement of women in the business or corporate world, but not at the expense of the home and family structure. One thing I have always appreciated about my bride, Dr. Angel Byrd, is that she is as professional and as progressive as they come, but our home and our children have always been a priority. Our children have never had to be latchkey kids because one of us has always been there for them. This really does make a difference in the confidence of your children. Our children have always had us available to reassure them of whom they are to us and who they are in Christ.

Chapter 15
Guilty! 5 to 10

⁴Marriage must be honored in every respect, with no cheating on the relationship, because God will judge the sexually immoral person and the person who commits adultery. Hebrews 13:4 Common English Bible (CEB)

Almost every time I hear someone talking about this passage, it is in reference to getting anything to go on sexually in a marriage. Sometimes men take this Scripture and try to force anything they can on their wives in the bedroom. They are usually trying to bring some of the things they experienced, saw or heard about in the world, into their marriage; and heaven forbid bringing it into a Godly marriage. The marriage bed is undefiled, however what defiles it is whoremongering and adulterous living. God never has and never will be ok with sex outside of marriage. I don't care what society practices today. It does not matter if they are the only person you are having sex with or if they have promised to marry you in the future. However you want to twist it, it is still twisted in the sight of God. I have heard people say that God understands, but what they are really saying when they talk or think like this, is that they don't understand God. The marriage is the only institution by which man has a legal right to sexual intercourse, and from there on a man who loves God and a woman who loves God should be able to agree on appropriate enjoyment in the sexual arena. Some of the things that are happening in the sexual arena today are so polluted, and engrafted from a man or woman's time in the world before Christ (B.C.) or Pre-Jesus (P.J.). Sex in the world is lust driven. No matter how much two people may think that they care for each other. Real love comes with real commitment. If your mind is not renewed, you'll have expectations for your marital sexual arena that come from before Christ or from when you were not living a godly life. This is common in most Christian marriages today, because so many people are not virgins when they say I do. When I say virgins, I don't just mean sexually but also virgins in what they've seen with their eyes and what they've allowed to take over their thoughts.

Personally, when I think about this passage of Scripture and I think about the days and times we are living in, I can't help think about how different things would be if there was a difference in the way we felt about adultery. Just think about it for a moment. If we took the marriage commitment seriously and maybe even enforced laws against adultery, what would some of the potential differences be in society? What if a person who was tried and proven guilty for adultery could be sentenced to prison time? I think there would be far less adultery in our society. You might be saying "Dr. Byrd, that is a bit harsh," but I would beg to differ. As a marriage counselor, I know that one of the toughest things many couples have had to deal with in their marriage is knowing that your spouse has cheated on you sexually. Some couples never get over this. Now I am aware that potential repercussions of such a law would seemingly mean that many people would just say no to marriage altogether, but that is only if we tried to institute something like this now. If this was something that would have been going on for the past 100 years we would see more couples actually trying to work out their differences instead of tipping out when there are differences. Adultery is one of the most egregious acts you can commit. It is downright nasty to share yourself with another in the way that you give yourself to your spouse. If you are married or considering marriage, I would suggest that you and your mate spend time in I Corinthians 13 so that you can operate in real love. Together you should talk about your options in the sexual arena; the marriage bed is undefiled, filled with love and passion for one another.

Chapter 16

Do What I say Woman!

¹Wives, likewise, submit to your own husbands. Do this so that even if some of them refuse to believe the word, they may be won without a word by their wives' way of life. ² After all, they will have observed the reverent and holy manner of your lives. ³ Don't try to make yourselves beautiful on the outside, with stylish hair or by wearing gold jewelry or fine clothes. ⁴ Instead, make yourselves beautiful on the inside, in your hearts, with the enduring quality of a gentle, peaceful spirit. This type of beauty is very precious in God's eyes.⁵ For it *was in this way that holy women who trusted in God used to make themselves beautiful, accepting the authority of their own husbands. ^{6} For example, Sarah accepted Abraham's authority when she called him master. You have become her children when you do well and don't respond to threats with fear. ^{7} Husbands, likewise, submit by living with your wife in ways that honor her, knowing that she is the weaker partner. Honor her all the more, as she is also a coheir of the gracious care of life. Do this so that your prayers won't be hindered.* 1 Peter 3:1-7 Common English Bible (CEB)

This is one of my favorite passages in the entire Bible. Why wouldn't it be? This passage allows us married men to get our wives to do whatever we want them to do. Right! That must be true, because I have heard men use this passage my whole life. It did not matter if the men had never read it in the Bible or actually heard it in church for themselves. They still used it as a Biblical truth for married men. It is amazing that men all over the world might use this passage to their benefit with such conviction, but would not pay too much attention to anything else the Bible has to say. Even if, this is what God is saying, and I'm not saying that it is, the fact that you would read His Word and then ignore His Word would disqualify you from receiving the benefits of it; from any sane woman, that is! Well anyone who actually knows or follows me, knows that I'm just kidding about why this would be my favorite passage in the Holy Scriptures! With that said, I do subscribe to wives submitting to their own husbands. I know this can get a little unpredictable. Some would say that a woman is only responsible for submitting to her husband if he is following God and submitting to God's word. I do believe that this was God's original intent for the marriage relationship. The man would submit to God and the wife would submit to her husband. However, if we leave it right there it kind of gives the wife the right to decide whether or not her husband is submitting to God and if she doesn't think that he is, she wouldn't be obligated to submit to him. Can't you see that this would be some dangerous and shaky ground, especially in today's society with this major independent spirit going on with women? That of course is one way to look at it, but another way is to believe that everyone is responsible for his or her own role in the Scriptures as it relates to God's expectations of you. So, since we're talking about wives right now, that would mean, the wife should submit to her own husband in order to please God and not based on her judgment of how well he is holding up to his role of submission. There, of course would have to be some measure of safety and precautions used with wisdom. A wife is definitely not going to submit to something crazy like her husband telling her to go outside of specific laws, principles and ways to live as described in the Word of God. There are husbands that try to bring other women into their marriage bed. That ain't God! There are husbands who try to get their wives to enjoy lustful pornography with them. That ain't God! There may even be husbands that try to entice their wives to shut off all of their family and friends in order to beat them down and mentally abuse them. You know that ain't God! I believe this is one of those passages of Scripture where we have to put our best efforts in to practice on how we interpret. We have to think about what God was originally saying. We have to combine it with other like Scriptures and put it all together. We also have to rely on the Holy Spirit to reveal God's heart to us. This is no time to run rampant on some new revelation that only you have, that no other scholar has seen it in the past 500 years. Let's recognize that there is a mouthful said in these seven verses, starting with a plan of action for women of God to win their unbelieving/backslidden husbands back to the Word of God. If your husband is not following the Word of God, you won't be able to win him with the Word of God.

I hope that this is just a season of backsliding and not a case where you have married an unbeliever. I know that no Christian that has given their life to the Lord Jesus Christ would give their hand in marriage to someone who rejects their Savior. That is worse than inviting someone to your house for dinner after they have just told you they cannot stand your children. It would not happen! So let us assume he is a Christian but just operating in a baby, carnal or immature stage. You will have to win him by your actions and your spirit and not by brow beating him with Scripture or with what your pastor has said during one of his sermons. The last thing he will want to hear is what another man has to say. Here is something to think about. Isn't it interesting that he didn't give instructions for a man of God to win an unbelieving woman or one who is not following the word of God? I would have to think that is because God knew that in most cases, a husband that is following God and God's Word, his wife would automatically also follow God. My Bishop, Dr. Steve Houpe would always say, "A man of God is not going to tolerate his wife and family not following him as he follows Christ." An example of a woman that submitted to her own husband in the way that would help you win your husband would be Sarah, whom the Bible says, obeyed Abraham and submitted to him and called him "Lord" which means "teacher". This is the daughter you can become if you act in such a manner. One of the greatest men of faith in our recent times was Smith Wigglesworth[4] whom was won over to the Lord by the submission that his wife took on when she became a believer. I do not know if you are ready for this but at one point Smith locked her out of the house because she came home late from an evening church service and this woman of God slept on the back stoop overnight. When Smith woke up the next morning to let her in, she promptly said, "Good morning and what would you like for breakfast." I know that just caused the hair on your head to stand up if this was the first time you heard that, but it just goes to show that God knows how to win someone better than we do.

---

[4] An early evangelist born in the 19th century who was a Pentecostal minister,

Now let us talk about verse seven, which is a wonderful verse. Husbands are instructed to dwell with our wives according to knowledge and to honor them as if we were honoring or taking care of something as precious as a priceless and gentle vessel. Could you imagine going to the White House and allowed to handle something that was precious, gentle, and easily breakable? You would handle it with much care and you would make sure to cradle it with both hands so that there would be no chance for you to break, dent, or even scratch it. Your wives are to be handled in such a way! Just writing this is making me want to step up my game as it relates to handling my wife. Sometimes if you have a strong, talented, and resourceful woman, you have a tendency to allow her to do more than she should have to do because she seems to be able to handle it. Even though she will do as much as you will let her do, she still is a female, and there is still something inside of her that would love to have you take care of it for her as much as you possibly can. Men you know that this capability to take care of her is in you. If you have to help an elderly woman, you do it with care, gentleness, and consideration. If she tries to do anything, you tell her, "just relax, I've got it." This is what your wife is looking for. Handle your wives in just the same manner as you would an older or priceless heirloom. I am not saying that you are old women; I am saying that you are priceless and valuable.

Chapter 17

Is It Love or Like?

⁴ Love is patient; love is kind, it isn't jealous, it doesn't brag, it isn't arrogant,⁵ it isn't rude, it doesn't seek its own advantage, it isn't irritable, it doesn't keep a record of complaints, ⁶ it isn't happy with injustice, but it is happy with the truth. ⁷ Love puts up with all things, trusts in all things, hopes for all things, endures all things. ⁸ Love never fails. As for prophecies, they will be brought to an end. As for tongues, they will stop. As for knowledge, it will be brought to an end. 1 Corinthians 13:4-8 Common English Bible (CEB)

What better way to come close to the end of this book by talking about love. These few Scriptures have put the 13th chapter of 1 Corinthians on the map as "The Love Chapter". I am convinced that it is utterly impossible to operate in this kind of love without being dominated in your thought life with the love of God. Today it is almost impossible for a Christian marriage to operate in this kind of love because the things of this world today dominate most Christians. I hear it all the time. A wife is very distraught with her husband and the way he treats her at home. When she mentions it to him, he comes up with some crazy train of thought that he heard on television or in a movie in which the couple ended up in a divorce. Some of the techniques used in problem solving today make no natural sense. The television has supplanted good sound Biblical advice. Even if you give someone good advice, and they acknowledge that it is good, when they try to use it, they don't have the discipline to replace the television knowledge with something that will actually work.

Another major hindrance to marriages operating in this kind of love is that nasty little four letter word that Satan pushes on us "Self." We will never be able to operate in the Agape love of God in our marriages as long as we are so hooked into ourselves. How do I look? What does everyone think about me? What if people think I'm being taken advantage of? Who cares what everybody else is thinking? To be very honest, other people are not thinking about you as much as you think they are because they are too busy thinking about themselves. The Bible describes it as the lust of the flesh, the lust of the eyes and the pride of life. God and His kind of love, is all about giving and what is in it for others. Love is not about what you have done for me lately; it is about how I can express more of this unselfish Godly love to you. Here is something for you; marriage should not be about competition with one another. Love is one place where it is all right to create healthy competition in your marriage. Compete to see who can love whom more. Compete to see who can serve whom more.

Compete to see who can forgive each other more. Compete to express love more and more. Just think about it; the Bible says love never fails. We can handle any failure within our marital relationship by either spouse, simply by operating in love. Yeah I know you say you love her and I know you say you love him, but the Bible is clear on the type of love it is referring too. This kind of Biblical love never fails. I believe couples that say they love each other but their marriage does not show it in manifestation, are not really loving each other at all but they care for each other. They once had loving feelings for one another and now that they have lost that loving feeling, it is more of them having invested so much time into each other. In some cases, they never really loved each other with God's kind of love. In other cases, they were overwhelmed with ecstasy and the chemicals that are released in all of us during that stage of the relationship. Unfortunately, for all of us, those chemicals fade away and real love at some point has to be developed. I believe this is a point that needs to be made that is often not made. I remember my Bishop telling me that when he married his sweet sugar cane from Louisiana, Dr. Donna L Houpe, he did not love her. He made a quality decision to marry her based on what he knew about her. He knew she was faithful in the house of God. He knew she was submitted to her Pastor. He knew she loved her son. He knew she preferred her son over herself. What all of these things led him to know was that he would eventually grow to have feelings for her, but whenever those feelings were not present, she would still be the one that he could make a conscious decision to love. Love is a choice and he made that choice to love her. If more believers would make the right choice and stand by it, more marriages would succeed. He also knew that if they would worship together, attend Bible study together, and pray together, there would be nothing they could not overcome in their marriage. I heard a very interesting statistic, which I believe to be true. In society, one out of every 2.5 marriages ends up in a divorce, but the odds change to 1 out of every 1,100 divorcing if the couples would do three things. When couples attend mid-week service together, pray together and study the Bible together, the odds of them divorcing would be overwhelmingly far and few between, especially compared to those who do not do those three things. What does a stat like that tell you? It tells me that marriage God's way is flawless and marriage the world's way is FLAWED.

Chapter 18
Marriage Only Works Through Obedience

²² Then Samuel replied, "Does the LORD want entirely burned offerings and sacrifices as much as obedience to the LORD? Listen to this: obeying is better than sacrificing, paying attention is better than fat from rams, 1 Samuel 15:22 Common English Bible (CEB)

I used to hear these words ringing in my ear as a young kid growing up; "Obedience is better than sacrifice." This statement seemed as if they were always the pre-curser to a spanking or they followed a spanking. I thought for sure I knew what this saying meant and one thing I knew was that I didn't want to be the sacrifice. Now, if this is what the saying meant, I spent most of my life knowing a truth from the Word of God. However, after studying the Word of God for myself, I have come to realize that I was way off in my thinking and so was everyone else I heard use those five words. The way I understood this phrase simply meant that if you would do what you were supposed to do, you would avoid trouble or the consequences that came with disobedience. However true this line of thinking may be, it is not what this phrase was saying in the Bible. I'm sure you can find other Scriptures to support the statement and the line of thinking which is a good way to think. If everyone in marriage would be obedient to the Word of God and obedient to the vows of marriage, they would avoid the sacrifices that come with disobedience. For example, your wedding vows proclaim exclusivity to this one individual. However, if you disobey the vows one can experience sexually transmitted diseases, children out of wedlock, divorce, orphaned children without both parents, and even losing what you've built financially. In that case, obedience would be better than disobedience. Therefore, by now, you're probably wondering why it sounds as if I'm saying this is not what the Bible was saying here in 1 Samuel, but it sounds like I am agreeing with the way it has been used for so many years. I guess you would be right and wrong in a way. Therefore, if that is the way you use it, that's o.k. as long as you don't quote it as being Biblical. What the Bible was saying had more to do with being obedient to God versus religious sacrifices as the lambs and goat's blood. This appears as if people knew that if they planned to sin and disobey, all one would need to do was to sacrifice to make up for sin. This reminds us of today's times. Whether or not you are a Christian using God's grace as your sacrifice or if you are Catholic and confession is your sacrifice; it does not matter. Many Christians and Catholics sin with the crutch of today's sacrifice in the back of their mind. I remember growing up in Catholic school through the 12th grade. I know confession was not intended by God to be used in the manner that I saw people using it. I would hear them say, "I'll just go to confession afterwards." In the same way, Christians today will say things like "God's grace is sufficient." This is what 1 Samuel: 15, verse 2 is referring to when it says "obedience is better than sacrifice." Now it did not say obedience was easier than sacrifice, but it did say that it was better than sacrifice. To obey God's ways in today's society takes discipline like never before. Obedience will have a direct result on what you believe, and what you believe will have a direct result on what you hear. The fact that everyone has a television and a cell phone available, leads to many distractions than in any other time in history. So many of us do not understand just how much we've been influenced by everything we are watching and listening to on these devices.

Watching and Listening

What we watch and what we hear has an impact on our daily lives. One day we are saying "I would never do that," and the next month we are doing exactly what we said we would not do. Maybe you were overheard saying that you would never say certain things in a matter of a few months, you are not only saying it but texting it, tweeting it and plastering it all over Facebook. You might ask, "Dr. Byrd "how does this happen?", and I would say you only have to look at how much time you are involved each day with activities such as social media. Now that will tweet! If you go to church a couple of hours a week and read a Scripture or two a day, that won't even come close to matching the five or six hours per day of television, social media, gossip, radio or your iPod. You are not giving yourself a fighting chance to align with God's Word! God says that this Book of the Law is what you meditate on day and night. The Bible is what should be your focus when you wake up, during lunch and dinner, and all of your daily activities. When I was a kid after school, a cartoon character would state, "You are what you eat from your head down to your feet. If this cartoon is true, the same goes for what you watch and listen to. You are what you hear. Another way of saying it would be; you are a result of your dominant thoughts and your thoughts are a result of what you hear most. Take this opporunity to be oebdient to the Word of God and avoid using the sacrifices of today's society.

Conclusion

As you can see from each chapter above, we all have flaws that limit the ability for us to express the God kind of love in our marriages. The more flaws you see, the more work you need to do on your marriage. It is my desire that as you have read this book you do not see your marriage as an insurmountable task but as a work in progress. With the necessary adjustments in knowledge, understanding, and wisdom, you can have the marriage that you dreamed about on your wedding day. Yes, you must do it the Manufacturer's way and not your own way.

As you reflect over what you have read, put the information into one of three categories. The first category is that of knowledge. Knowledge is defined as facts, information, and skills acquired by a person through experience or education; the theoretical or practical understanding of a subject. Ask yourself what parts of this book was new information for me. If it was new information, begin to dissect it until you have a full grasp of what it is saying and what God is saying to you. The second category would be that of understanding. Understanding is defined as the ability to understand or comprehend something. Another way to look at it is being sympathetically aware of other people's feelings; tolerant and forgiving. Ask yourself if you've had knowledge of this material but maybe lacked understanding on some of it. Whatever parts you did not have true understanding of, please dissect it a little deeper to make sure that you now have the full understanding of it. I always know if I understand something if I can teach it to someone else. Can you teach the lessons laid out before you in this writing? The third category I want you to put it into would be that of wisdom. The definition of Wisdom is as the soundness of an action or decision with regard to the application of experience, knowledge, and good judgment. Better yet, do you do what you know? This is the tricky category for most of us. You see we can know some things and we can even understand some things but wisdom is operating in what we know in the heat of the battle. You see I may have knowledge of some things as it relates to the stock market and financial industry. I have read many books and magazine articles. I have attended many seminars on finances and investing. I may even understand a lot of it with the ability to teach it to a novice. The tricky part is do I personally operate in it on a regular basis in my own personal finances. If so, I would probably be financially well off or a multi-millionaire by now. It is the same for you as it relates to your marriage. You may have read this book and said, "I know all of the information in this book and I tell others about it all of the time." My question to you is, how has that been working for you up to this point in your marriage?

The successful, flourishing marriages are the ones that operate in wisdom as it relates to the knowledge and understanding they have in marriage. If you want to know how wise you are in marriage, all you have to do is ask your spouse. If they are not afraid to tell you the truth, that would be the best answer to your question. It is amazing how wise we can be at other things in life but not in our marriage. Some of you are running fortune 500 companies, successful entrepreneurs, Pastors of great ministries, Real-estate tycoons, corporate supervisors, and stay at home mothers and you do it very well. If we could get you to achieve the same success in marriage as you have in your career the world would be a much better place. There is a reason that you are successful in your career and the same effort and energy you put into becoming successful at one is the same thing it takes to become successful at the other. Imagine being at your work place and watching two adults argue over their opinion to the point of screaming or even using profanity. Then one of them storms off and leaves the room or the building. They come to work every day for the next couple of weeks and do not even talk to each other. Wouldn't you say that was childish, immature, or unprofessional at the least? Before you agree with me, look in to your marriage and see if those are the actions that are displayed when you don't get your way or when you disagree with each other. If this is how you act at home, it is just as childish and immature as it would be for professionals in the workplace. It is time to grow up. It is time to rid your marriage of the flaws that are hindering your relationship.

We have been counseling married couples for many years and what we have come to realize is that people are trying to do marriage without putting an importance on self-growth and enhancement. You are no good for someone else when you have a trunk full of issues tucked away from your past. If you can get in touch with your own hurts, fears and insecurities, you'll have a chance to heal and move on from them. Most of all the people we see in our counseling practice are as surprised as a birthday party they knew nothing about when these things are brought to the session. Many are often times able to see them in their spouse, but never in themselves. We tend to attribute our faults to the actions of our spouse, not realizing that our faults are our faults whether we're with them or with someone else. Our hurts, fears and insecurities travel with us everywhere we go. The only way to get rid of them is to give them to God. When we try to protect ourselves, we act as our own God. It would be better to give them over to the one true wise God and allow Him to protect us. When we try to protect ourselves, we wind up hurting other people and usually the ones closest to us. That is why we inflict the most pain on our spouse. It is usually not intentional, but comes out of a coping mechanism developed over the years that is intended to keep us from being hurt.

I am asking you for the sake of your marriage and family to let it all out. You must first acknowledge them. Second, you must confess them to God. Third, you must confess them to someone else. The perfect person would be your spouse. For some of you, that may need to start out being a counselor. Whomever you trust that to be, it is necessary to get the release needed to move forward and to stop hurting the ones you love.

I pray that Flawed has done as much for you as it has for me in writing it. Please encourage others to go out and purchase a copy for themselves and for their marriage. We can never get enough good information on marriage in the times we are living in. Our prayer is that God may bless you and your marriage!

References

[i] Matthew 18: 22, forgive seven times seventy times.
[ii] American Psychological Association, Marriage and Divorce, http://www.apa.org/topics/divorce/, Accessed November 11, 2014
[iii] Centers for Disease Control, http://www.cdc.gov/nchs/mardiv.htm, accessed November 10, 2014
[iv] Centers for Disease Control, Marriages and Divorce, http://www.cdc.gov/nchs/mardiv.htm, Accessed November 11, 2014
[v] Banshich, Mark, in The Intelligent Divorce, The High Failure Rate of Second and Third Marriages; Why are second and third marriages more likely to fail? Psychology Today, http://www.psychologytoday.com/blog/the-intelligent-divorce/201202/the-high-failure-rate-second-and-third-marriages

Gerald Rogers, You have one Life to Live, Live Big, accessed September 26, 2014, http://geraldrogers.com/marriage-advice-i-wish-i-would-have-had/

www.ingramcontent.com/pod-product-compliance
Lightning Source LLC
Chambersburg PA
CBHW071425160426
43195CB00013B/1806